THE
BHAGAVAD GITA

THE LORD'S SONG

Annie Besant

Table of Contents

Introduction to the Bhagavad Gita

The Bhagavad Gita is one of the most revered spiritual texts in the world, a Hindu scripture that also offers profound insights into self-realization, duty, and the pursuit of wisdom. Across centuries, its teachings have inspired saints, philosophers, and leaders, providing insights into both the material and spiritual dimensions of life.

This edition presents the **classic translation by Annie Besant**, a scholar and theosophist who dedicated her life to understanding and sharing the profound teachings of the East. Alongside her translation, you will find **a chapter-by-chapter commentary**, offering both spiritual insights and practical applications of Krishna's wisdom. Whether you are approaching the *Gita* as a spiritual seeker, a philosopher, or someone looking for guidance in modern life, this book will serve as a companion on your journey.

The Bhagavad Gita and Its Place in the Mahabharata

The *Bhagavad Gita* is a part of the great Hindu epic, the *Mahabharata*, which is one of the longest and most influential epics in world literature. Composed over several centuries, the *Mahabharata* narrates the complex history of two feuding branches of the Kuru dynasty—the **Pandavas** and the **Kauravas**—who battle for the throne of Hastinapura.

The *Mahabharata* is not just a historical account but a deeply philosophical and spiritual text, addressing themes of duty (dharma), righteousness, fate, and devotion. The *Bhagavad Gita* appears in the Bhishma Parva (Book 6) of the *Mahabharata*, just before the great war of Kurukshetra begins. It is in this moment of impending battle that Krishna, the divine charioteer, imparts his timeless wisdom to Arjuna, framing the Gita as both a dialogue and a spiritual guide for all humanity.

At the heart of the *Bhagavad Gita* lies a deep exploration of **duty (dharma), selfless action (karma yoga), devotion (bhakti yoga), and knowledge (jnana yoga)**. The text is set on the battlefield of Kurukshetra, where a great war unfolds between two factions of the same royal family—the Pandavas and the Kauravas. This war arises from a long-standing conflict over the throne of Hastinapura, marked by political intrigue, betrayal, and

3

injustice. Despite being the rightful heirs, the Pandavas were denied their kingdom by their cousins, the Kauravas, leading to an inevitable confrontation.

Arjuna, a prince of the Pandava family and one of the greatest warriors, finds himself paralyzed by doubt and moral conflict as he prepares to engage in battle. He surveys the battlefield and sees among his opponents his own kin, revered elders, and beloved teachers. Overcome with despair, he questions the righteousness of war and struggles with his duty as a Kshatriya (warrior class) to fight for justice. In this moment of inner turmoil, he turns to Krishna, his charioteer and divine guide, seeking clarity and wisdom. This conversation between Arjuna and Krishna forms the essence of the *Bhagavad Gita*, offering profound teachings on duty, righteousness, and the nature of reality.

It is at this pivotal moment that **Krishna**, Arjuna's charioteer and an incarnation of the divine, reveals the eternal truths of existence. Over eighteen chapters, Krishna systematically addresses Arjuna's confusion, delivering profound teachings on various paths to liberation:

- **Karma Yoga (Path of Selfless Action):** Performing one's duty without attachment to personal gain.

- **Bhakti Yoga (Path of Devotion):** Surrendering to the divine with unwavering faith.

- **Jnana Yoga (Path of Knowledge):** Seeking ultimate truth through wisdom and introspection.

- **Dhyana Yoga (Path of Meditation):** Cultivating inner stillness to perceive reality beyond the material world.

Metaphysical Foundations of the Bhagavad Gita

A fundamental teaching of the *Bhagavad Gita* is the relationship between Atman (the individual soul) and Brahman (the Supreme Reality). Krishna explains that the Atman is eternal, beyond birth and death, and that the material world is Maya (illusion)—a temporary, ever-changing existence that veils the true nature of reality. To transcend this illusion, one must cultivate spiritual wisdom (jnana) and act with detachment, recognizing that the soul is distinct from the body and beyond worldly suffering.

Krishna urges Arjuna to see himself not as a mere physical being, but as an immortal soul (Atman) temporarily inhabiting a human form. Through devotion and knowledge, one can realize unity with Brahman, escaping the cycle of birth and rebirth (samsara) and attaining Moksha (liberation).

One of the most awe-inspiring moments in the *Bhagavad Gita* occurs when Krishna reveals his Vishvarupa (Universal Form) to Arjuna. This vision is overwhelming—Arjuna sees Krishna as the infinite, all-encompassing cosmic presence, containing the entire universe within himself. He perceives countless divine forms, celestial beings, and the inexorable march of time itself. The vision is both beautiful and terrifying, symbolizing Krishna's supreme power as the ultimate reality (Para-Brahman).

This moment reinforces the idea that Krishna is not just a guide or teacher but the very fabric of existence itself. It also serves as a turning point for Arjuna, who finally understands Krishna's divine nature and his role within the cosmic order. This revelation humbles Arjuna, compelling him to surrender completely to Krishna's will.

The Concept of Dharma

The concept of **Dharma (duty/righteousness)** is central to the *Bhagavad Gita*, but it exists on multiple levels. Krishna clarifies that Dharma is not a rigid, one-size-fits-all rule but a dynamic principle that depends on one's role, circumstances, and spiritual evolution. The Gita presents four key types of Dharma:

- **Sanatana Dharma (Eternal Duty):** The universal, eternal laws of righteousness that apply to all beings, such as truth, non-violence, and devotion to the divine.

- **Varnashrama Dharma (Social and Occupational Duty):** Duties based on one's caste and stage of life, which, in Arjuna's case, means fulfilling his role as a warrior (Kshatriya).

- **Sva-Dharma (Personal Duty):** The unique responsibilities of an individual based on their circumstances, talents, and obligations.

- **Parama-Dharma (Supreme Duty):** The highest duty—surrendering to God and acting in alignment with divine will, transcending worldly obligations.

Krishna resolves Arjuna's moral dilemma by explaining that acting according to Sva-Dharma, even when difficult, is better than following another's path, as it aligns with one's inherent nature. He further teaches that the highest form of Dharma is complete surrender to the divine (Bhakti Yoga)—acting not for personal gain but as an offering to Krishna himself.

Annie Besant's Translation

Annie Besant was a pioneering theosophist, social reformer, and spiritual teacher who devoted herself to studying the wisdom traditions of India. Her translation of the *Bhagavad Gita* is both faithful to the Sanskrit text and accessible to Western readers, making it a valuable resource for those seeking a deeper understanding of this scripture. Unlike many other versions, her work captures the philosophical and mystical essence of the text, rather than being only a purely literal translation.

This edition preserves her original translation while adding commentary that clarifies key themes and makes the teachings even more relevant for today's readers. It is structured to maximize both spiritual depth and practical application, making it useful for a wide audience:

1. **Each chapter begins with a commentary** that provides context, explains core ideas, and highlights key lessons.

2. **The original translation by Annie Besant follows,** allowing you to experience the text in its classical form.

If you are reading the *Bhagavad Gita* for the first time, take your time with each chapter. Reflect on Krishna's teachings and consider how they relate to your own journey. For those revisiting the text, this edition will provide fresh perspectives that deepen your understanding.

PREFACE

BY ANNIE BESANT

AMONG the priceless teachings that may be found in the great Hindu poem of the *Mahâbhârata*, there is none so rare and precious as this—"The Lord's Song." Since it fell from the divine lips of Shrî Krishna on the field of battle, and stilled the surging emotions of his disciple and friend, how many troubled hearts has it quieted and strengthened, how many weary souls has it led to Him! It is meant to lift the aspirant from the lower levels of renunciation, where objects are renounced, to the loftier heights where desires are dead, and where the Yogi dwells in calm and ceaseless contemplation, while his body and mind are actively employed in discharging the duties that fall to his lot in life. That the spiritual man need not be a recluse, that union with the divine Life may be achieved and maintained in the midst of worldly affairs, that the obstacles to that union lie not outside us but within us—such is the central lesson of the Bhagavad-Gita.

It is a scripture of Yoga; now Yoga is literally union, and it means harmony with the divine Law, the becoming one with the divine Life, by the subdual of all outward-going energies. To reach this, balance must be gained, equilibrium, so that the self, joined to the Self, shall not be affected by pleasure or pain, desire or aversion, or any of the "pairs of opposites" between which untrained selves swing backwards and forwards. Moderation is therefore the keynote of the Gita, and the harmonising of all the constituents of man, till they vibrate in perfect attunement with the One, the Supreme Self. This is the aim the disciple is to set before him. He must learn not to be attracted by the attractive, nor repelled by the repellent, but must see both as manifestations of the one Lord, so that they may be lessons for his guidance, not fetters for his bondage. In the midst of turmoil he must rest in the Lord of Peace, discharging every duty to the fullest, not because he seeks the results of his actions, but because it is his duty to perform them. His heart is an altar, love to his Lord the flame burning upon it; all his acts, physical and mental, are sacrifices offered on the altar; and once offered, he has with them no further concern.

7

As though to make the lesson more impressive, it was given on a field of battle. Arjuna, the warrior-prince, was to vindicate his brother's title, to destroy a usurper who was oppressing the land; it was his duty as prince, as warrior, to fight for the deliverance of his nation and to restore order and peace. To make the contest more bitter, loved comrades and friends stood on both sides, wringing his heart with personal anguish, and making a conflict of duties as well as physical strife. Could he slay those to whom he owed love and duty, and trample on ties of kindred? To break family ties was a sin; to leave the people in cruel bondage was a sin; where was the right way? Justice must be done, else law would be disregarded; but how slay without sin? The answer is the burden of the book: Have no personal interest in the event; carry out the duty imposed by the position in life, realise that Ishvara, at once Lord and Law is the doer, working out the mighty evolution that ends in bliss and peace; be identified with Him by devotion, and then perform duty as duty, fighting without passion or desire, without anger or hatred; thus activity forges no bonds, Yoga is accomplished and the soul is free.

Such is the obvious teaching of this sacred book. But as all the acts of an Avatâra are symbolical, we may pass from the outer to the inner planes, and see in the fight of Kurukshetra the battlefield of the soul, and in the sons of Dhritarâshtra enemies it meets in its progress; Arjuna becomes the type of the struggling soul of the disciple, and Shrî Krishna is the Logos of the soul. Thus the teaching of the ancient battlefield gives guidance in all later days, and trains the aspiring soul in treading the steep and thorny path that leads to peace. To all such souls in East and West come these divine lessons, for the path is one, though it has many names, and all souls seek the same goal, though they may not realise their unity.

In order to preserve the precision of the Sanskrit, a few technical terms have been given in the original in foot-notes; Manah is the mind, both in the lower mental processes in which it is swayed by the senses, by passions and emotions, and in the higher processes of reasoning; Buddhi is the faculty above the ratiocinating mind, and is the Pure Reason, exercising the discriminative faculty of intuition, of spiritual discernment; if these original words are not known to the reader, the Bhagavad-Gita loses much of its practical value as a treatise on Yoga, and the would-be learner becomes confused.

The epithets applied to Shrî Krishna and Arjuna—the variety of which is so characteristic of Sanskrit conversation—are for the most part left untranslated, as being musical they thus add to the literary charm, whereas the genius of English is so different from that of Sanskrit, that the many-footed epithets become sometimes almost grotesque in translation. Names derived from that of an ancestor, as Pârtha, meaning the son of Prithâ, Kaunteya, meaning the son of Kuntî, are used in one form or the other, according to the rhythm of the sentence. One other trifling matter, which is yet not trifling, if it aids the student: when Atmâ means the One Self, the Self of all, it is printed in small capitals; where it means the lower, the personal self, it is printed in ordinary type; this is done because there is sometimes a play on the word, and it is difficult for an untrained reader to follow the meaning without some such assistance. The word Brahman, the One, the Supreme, is throughout translated the "Eternal." The word "Deva," literally "Shining One," is thus translated throughout. The use of the Western word "God" alike for "Brahman" and for the "Devas" is most misleading; the Hindu never uses the one for the other, and never blurs the unity of the Supreme by the multiplicity of ministering Intelligences.

My wish, in adding this translation to those already before the public, was to preserve the spirit of the original, especially in its deeply devotional tone, while at the same time giving an accurate translation, reflecting the strength and the terseness of the Sanskrit. In order that mistakes, due to my imperfect knowledge, might be corrected, all of this translation has passed through the hands of one or other of the following gentlemen—friends of mine at Benares—to whom I here tender my grateful acknowledgments: Bâbus Pramada Das Mitra, Gangânath Jhâ, Kâli Charan Mitra, and Upendranath Basu. A few of the notes are also due to them. In the third and fourth editions I have also been much helped by Bâbu Bhagavân Dâs, to whom I add my cordial thanks.

ANNIE BESANT.

FIRST DISCOURSE

Context & Setting

Chapter 1 of the *Bhagavad Gita*, known as the *Arjuna Vishada Yoga* (The Yoga of Arjuna's Dejection), sets the stage for the entire dialogue between Arjuna and Krishna. The setting is the battlefield of **Kurukshetra**, where the great war between the Pandavas and the Kauravas is about to begin. The two armies stand poised for battle, and **Sanjaya**, the narrator of the *Mahabharata*, describes the scene to King **Dhritarashtra**, the blind ruler of Hastinapura.

As the battle is about to commence, **Duryodhana**, the leader of the Kauravas, approaches his commander, **Dronacharya**, and expresses his confidence and concerns regarding the opposing forces. This section highlights Duryodhana's political cunning and his fear of the Pandavas' strength despite his bravado.

Krishna, serving as Arjuna's charioteer, is then asked by Arjuna to place their chariot in the middle of the battlefield so he can see who he is about to fight. This seemingly simple request marks the beginning of Arjuna's deep inner conflict.

Arjuna's Moral Dilemma

As Arjuna surveys the battlefield, he becomes overwhelmed with sorrow and doubt. He sees before him his relatives, teachers, and dear friends—all of whom he must fight against. His heart sinks as he realizes the gravity of the battle ahead. He expresses his anguish to Krishna, lamenting that engaging in this war will bring destruction to his family, the collapse of dharma (righteousness), and moral ruin. Arjuna fears that by killing his own kin, he will be responsible for the downfall of his lineage and the erosion of sacred traditions. His attachment to his family blinds him to his duty as a warrior.

This moment is significant because it encapsulates the universal human struggle between duty and emotion, righteousness and attachment. Arjuna, once fearless, loses all resolve and declares that he will not fight. In despair, he throws down his bow and collapses, signaling his complete surrender to his inner turmoil. His reluctance highlights the complexity of dharma, the principle of duty that governs righteousness. For Arjuna, following his warrior dharma means waging war, yet his heart recoils at the idea of killing those he loves. His hesitation represents a broader philosophical struggle: should one adhere to duty at all costs, or should personal morality take precedence over societal obligations?

The Deeper Meaning Behind Arjuna's Struggle

The battlefield of Kurukshetra serves as a metaphor for the internal battle that all individuals face at some point in their lives. It represents the confrontation between personal desires and higher duties, between ego-driven emotions and the pursuit of righteousness. Arjuna's sorrow, though deeply personal, symbolizes the broader human condition of moral conflict. His paralysis is not mere cowardice but a profound existential crisis, one that mirrors the struggles faced by spiritual seekers and ethical thinkers throughout history.

At the heart of Arjuna's crisis is the illusion of loss. He perceives the destruction of his family and traditions as an irreparable tragedy, but this grief is rooted in attachment and ignorance. Later, Krishna will reveal the eternal nature of the soul, teaching that life and death are mere transitions in the grand scheme of existence. This perspective challenges Arjuna's emotional turmoil and urges him to adopt a vision beyond the material realm.

Arjuna's refusal to fight is an essential precursor to the *Bhagavad Gita*'s teachings. His despair compels him to seek guidance, marking the beginning of his transformation. Surrendering to Krishna, though stemming from hopelessness, is the first step toward wisdom. Only by acknowledging his confusion can he become receptive to divine insight. This turning point highlights a key lesson: before one can truly understand dharma, one must transcend the limitations of worldly attachments and fear.

Lead-In to Krishna's Teachings

As Chapter 1 draws to a close, Krishna remains silent, allowing Arjuna to voice his concerns fully before offering guidance. This moment is crucial because it demonstrates the necessity of self-reflection before one can receive wisdom. Just as in life, moments of deep crisis often precede moments of profound clarity. Krishna does not interrupt or rush to offer solutions but instead lets Arjuna express his grief, preparing him for the revelations to come.

Chapter 1, though lacking Krishna's direct teachings, is foundational to the *Bhagavad Gita*'s philosophical discourse. It establishes the central question of duty and righteousness that Krishna will later address. The scene of Arjuna's despair is not just about a warrior hesitating before battle—it is about the fundamental human need to reconcile action with ethics, responsibility with compassion, and personal loss with a greater cosmic order.

As we move into Chapter 2, Krishna will begin his discourse, dispelling Arjuna's doubts and offering the first of many teachings on self-realization, detachment, and the path to dharma. But before wisdom can be imparted, there must first be a willingness to listen. Arjuna's surrender at the end of Chapter 1 is that crucial first step—an admission of uncertainty that opens the door to true spiritual awakening.

Dhritarâshtra said:

On the holy plain, on the field of Kuru,[1] gathered together, eager for battle, what did they, O Sanjaya, my people and the Pândavas?(1)

Sanjaya said:

Having seen arrayed the army of the Pândavas, the Prince Duryodhana approached his teacher,[2] and spake these words:(2)

"Behold this mighty host of the sons of Pându, O teacher, arrayed by the son of Drupada, thy wise disciple.(3)

Heroes are these, mighty bowmen, to Bhîma and Arjuna equal in battle: Yuyudhâna, Virâta, and Drupada of the great car.[3] (4)

---

[1] The common ancestor of the contending parties, the Kurus and the Pândavas, in the impending battle.
[2] Drona, the son of Bharadvâja.
[3] One able to fight alone ten thousand bowmen.

Drishtaketu, Chekitâna and the valiant King of Kâshi, Purujit and Kuntibhoja, and Shaivya, bull[4] among men;(5)

Yudhâmanyu the strong, and Uttamaujas the brave; Saubhadra[5] and the Draupadeyas,[6] all of great cars.(6)

Know further all those who are our chiefs, O best of the twice-born, the leaders of my army; these I name to thee for thy information:(7)

Thou, Lord, and Bhîshma, and Karna and Kripa, conquering in battle; Ashvatthâmâ, Vikarna, and Saumadatti[7] also;(8)

And many others, heroes, for my sake renouncing their lives, with divers weapons and missiles, and all well-skilled in war.(9)

Yet insufficient seems this army of ours, though marshalled by Bhîshma, while that army of theirs seems sufficient, though marshalled by Bhîma;[8] (10)

Therefore in the rank and file let all, standing firmly in their respective divisions, guard Bhîshma, even all ye generals.(11)

To enhearten him, the Ancient of the Kurus, the Grandsire,[9] the glorious, blew his conch, sounding on high a lion's roar.(12)

Then conches and kettledrums, tabors and drums and cowhorns, suddenly blared forth, and the sound was tumultuous.(13)

Then, stationed in their great war-chariot, yoked to white horses, Mâdhava[10] and the son of Pându[11] blew their divine conches.(14)

---

[4] The bull, as the emblem of manly strength and vigour, is often used as an epithet of honour.
[5] Abhimanyu, the son of Subhadrâ and Arjuna.
[6] The sons and grandsons of Drupada.
[7] The son of Somadatta.
[8] The commentators differ in their interpretation of this verse; Anandagiri takes it to mean just the reverse of Shridhara Svâmi, "aparyâptam" being taken by the one as "insufficient," by the other as "unlimited."
[9] Bhishma.
[10] Shri Krishna.
[11] Arjuna.

Pânchajanya by Hrishîkesha, and Devadatta by Dhananjaya.[12] Vrikodara[13] of terrible deeds blew his mighty conch, Paundra;(15)

The King Yudhishthira, the son of Kuntî, blew Anantavijaya; Nakula and Sahadeva, Sughosha and Manipushpaka.[14] (16)

And Kâshya,[15] of the great bow and Shikhandî, the mighty car-warrior, Drishtadyumna and Virâta and Sâtyaki, the unconquered.(17)

Drupada and the Draupadeyas, O Lord of earth, and Saubhadra, the mighty-armed, on all sides their several conches blew.(18)

That tumultuous uproar rent the hearts of the sons of Dhritarâshtra, filling the earth and sky with sound.(19)

Then, beholding the sons of Dhritarâshtra standing arrayed, and flight of missiles about to begin, he whose crest is an ape, the son of Pându, took up his bow,(20)

And spake this word to Hrishîkesha, O Lord of Earth:

Arjuna said:

In the midst, between the two armies, stay my chariot, O Achyuta,[16] (21)

That I may behold these standing, longing for battle, with whom I must strive in this outbreaking war,(22)

And gaze on those here gathered together ready to fight, desirous of pleasing in battle the evil-minded son of Dhritarâshtra.(23)

Sanjaya said:

---

[12] Pânchajanya, Shri Krishna's conch, was made from the bones of the giant Panchajana, slain by him. The title Hrishîkesha is "Lord of the senses." Dhananjaya, the "conqueror of wealth," is a title often given to Arjuna, whose conch is the "God-given."
[13] Bhîma; the meaning of the name of his conch is doubtful.
[14] The conches of the remaining three brothers were named respectively "endless victory," "honey-tone," and "jewel-blossom."
[15] The King of Kâshi, the modern Benares.
[16] The changeless, the immovable.

Thus addressed by Gudâkesha,[17] Hrishîkesha, O Bhârata, having stayed that best of chariots in the midst, between the two armies,(24)

Over against Bhîshma, Drona and all the rulers of the world, said: "O Pârtha, behold these Kurus gathered together."(25)

Then saw Pârtha standing there, uncles and grandfathers, teachers, mother's brothers, cousins, sons and grandsons, comrades,(26)

Fathers-in-law and benefactors also in both armies; seeing all these kinsmen thus standing arrayed, Kaunteya,[18] (27)

Deeply moved to pity, thus uttered in sadness:

Arjuna said:

Seeing these my kinsmen, O Krishna, arrayed, eager to fight,(28)

My limbs fail and my mouth is parched, my body quivers, and my hair stands on end,(29)

Gândîva slips from my hand, and my skin burns all over, I am not able to stand, my mind is whirling,(30)

And I see adverse omens, O Keshava.[19] Nor do I foresee any advantage from slaying kinsmen in battle.(31)

For I desire not victory, O Krishna, nor kingdom, nor pleasures; what is kingdom to us, O Govinda, what enjoyment or even life?(32)

Those for whose sake we desire kingdom, enjoyments and pleasures, they stand here in battle, abandoning life and riches—(33)

Teachers, fathers, sons, as well as grandfathers, mother's brothers, fathers-in-law, grandsons, brothers-in-law, and other relatives.(34)

These I do not wish to kill, though myself slain, O Madhusûdana,[20] even for the sake of the kingship of the three worlds; how then for earth?(35)

---

[17] The lord of sleep, Arjuna.
[18] The son of Kuntî, Arjuna.
[19] "He who has luxurious hair," or, "He who sleeps on the waters."
[20] The slayer of Madhu, a demon.

Slaying these sons of Dhritarâshtra, what pleasure can be ours, O Janârdana?[21] Killing these desperadoes, sin will but take hold of us.(36)

Therefore we should not kill the sons of Dhritarâshtra, our relatives; for how, killing our kinsmen, may we be happy, O Mâdhava?(37)

Although these, with intelligence overpowered by greed, see no guilt in the destruction of a family, no crime in hostility to friends,(38)

Why should not we learn to turn away from such a sin, O Janârdana, who see the evils in the destruction of a family?(39)

In the destruction of a family the immemorial family traditions[22] perish; in the perishing of tradition, lawlessness overcomes the whole family;(40)

Owing to predominance of lawlessness, O Krishna, the women of the family become corrupt; women corrupted, O Vârshneya,[23] there ariseth caste confusion;(41)

This confusion draggeth to hell the slayers of the family, and the family; for their ancestors fall, deprived of rice-balls and libations.(42)

By these caste-confusing misdeeds of the slayers of the family, the everlasting caste customs[24] and family customs[24] are abolished.(43)

The abode of the men whose family customs[24] are extinguished, O Janârdana, is everlastingly in hell. Thus have we heard.(44)

Alas! in committing a great sin are we engaged, we who are endeavouring to kill our kindred from greed of the pleasures of kingship.(45)

If the sons of Dhritarâshtra, weapon in hand, should slay me, unresisting, unarmed, in the battle, that would for me be the better.(46)

Sanjaya said:

---

[21] "Destroyer of the people." Shri Krishna as the warrior conquering all forms of evil.

[22] Dharma; this is a wide word, primarily meaning the essential nature of a thing, that which makes it to be what it is externally: hence, the laws of its being, its duty: and it includes religious rites, appropriate to those laws, customs, also righteousness.

[23] Belonging to the family of Vrishni.

[24] Dharma.

Having thus spoken on the battle-field, Arjuna sank down on the seat of the chariot, casting away his bow and arrow, his mind overborne by grief.(47)

Thus in the glorious Upanishads of the Bhagavad-Gita, the science of the Eternal, the scripture of Yoga, the dialogue between Shri Krishna and Arjuna, the first discourse, entitled:

THE DESPONDENCY OF ARJUNA.

SECOND DISCOURSE

Krishna's Response to Arjuna's Despair

Chapter 2 of the *Bhagavad Gita*, known as *Sankhya Yoga* (The Yoga of Knowledge), marks the beginning of Krishna's teachings to Arjuna. While Chapter 1 ended with Arjuna consumed by grief and moral confusion, Chapter 2 introduces the first step toward wisdom—detachment and self-knowledge. Here, Krishna reprimands Arjuna's weakness, urging him to abandon his despair and fulfill his duty as a warrior. This moment represents a major shift in the *Gita*—from emotional turmoil to philosophical clarity.

Krishna challenges Arjuna's lamentation, declaring that true wisdom lies in understanding the eternal nature of the soul (Atman). He teaches that birth and death are mere transitions and that the soul itself is indestructible. By clinging to worldly attachments, Arjuna is clouded by illusion (*Maya*), preventing him from seeing his dharma clearly. Krishna's first lesson is thus one of self-realization and perspective—urging Arjuna to rise above his fears and act with unwavering commitment.

The Eternal Soul: Atman Beyond Birth and Death

One of the most famous teachings of the *Bhagavad Gita* emerges in this chapter: the distinction between the physical body and the immortal soul (Atman). Krishna explains that just as one discards old clothes and wears new ones, so too does the soul shed one body and take another. This teaching is a cornerstone of Vedantic thought, reinforcing the idea that suffering, fear, and attachment stem from identifying with the temporary body rather than the eternal self.

This idea is meant to liberate Arjuna from sorrow. By realizing that no one is truly born or dies, but instead moves through different states of existence, Arjuna should not grieve over the inevitable. Krishna's emphasis on detachment does not imply apathy but rather a shift in perspective—one that allows an individual to act without fear or hesitation.

The Philosophy of Action: Dharma and Nishkama Karma

Krishna then introduces **the importance of duty (dharma)**, particularly the warrior's responsibility to uphold righteousness. He reminds Arjuna that as a Kshatriya (warrior class), it is his sacred duty to fight for justice.

Krishna introduces the concept of Nishkama Karma (selfless action)—the idea that one must act without attachment to results. This is one of the central teachings of the *Gita*, advocating for action driven by duty rather than desire. Acting without selfish motives ensures that one remains spiritually balanced, unaffected by success or failure. This philosophy lays the foundation for Karma Yoga (the Yoga of Action), which Krishna will elaborate on in later chapters.

Self-Mastery Through Wisdom: Sankhya and Yoga

Krishna presents two primary paths to spiritual growth—**Jnana Yoga (the Path of Knowledge)** and **Karma Yoga (the Path of Action)**. He asserts that true wisdom (*Sankhya*) is understanding the eternal truth of existence, while disciplined action (*Yoga*) ensures that wisdom is applied in life. These paths are not mutually exclusive; rather, they work together. Knowledge alone is meaningless without action, and action without wisdom leads to confusion.

Krishna urges Arjuna to cultivate equanimity (Samatva)—the ability to remain steady and unshaken by success or failure. This mental discipline is essential to spiritual liberation (Moksha). By transcending dualities such as pleasure and pain, gain and loss, one attains true peace.

Arjuna's First Step Toward Spiritual Clarity

Chapter 2 is a turning point in the *Bhagavad Gita*. Arjuna, though still hesitant, begins to grasp the depth of Krishna's teachings. This chapter lays the foundation for the rest of the *Gita*, introducing key concepts that Krishna will expand upon. The realization that one's duty must be fulfilled with detachment and wisdom sets the stage for deeper discussions on devotion, renunciation, and self-discipline in the chapters to come.

Krishna's final message in this discourse is clear: act with unwavering focus, free from attachment, and surrender to the greater cosmic order. This is the path of the wise—the path to liberation.

Sanjaya said:

To him thus with pity overcome, with smarting brimming eyes, despondent, Madhusûdana spake these words:(1)

The Blessed Lord said:

Whence hath this dejection befallen thee in this perilous strait, ignoble[1], heaven-closing[2], infamous, O Arjuna?(2)

Yield not to impotence, O Partha! it doth not befit thee. Shake off this paltry faint-heartedness! Stand up, Parantapa![3] (3)

Arjuna said:

How, O Madhusûdana, shall I attack Bhîshma and Drona with arrows in battle, they who are worthy of reverence, O slayer of foes?(4)

Better in this world to eat even the beggar's crust than to slay these most noble Gurus. Slaying these Gurus, our well-wishers,[4] I should taste of blood-besprinkled feasts.(5)

Nor know I which for us be the better, that we conquer them or they conquer us—these, whom having slain we should not care to live, even these arrayed against us, the sons of Dhritarâshtra.(6)

My heart is weighed down with the vice of faintness; my mind is confused as to duty.[5] I ask thee which may be the better—that tell me decisively. I am thy disciple, suppliant to Thee; teach me.(7)

For I see not that it would drive away this anguish that withers up my senses, if I should attain unrivalled monarchy on earth, or even the sovereignty of the Shining Ones.(8)

Sanjaya said:

---

[1] Literally, un-âryan.
[2] Literally, non-svargan: cowardice in the warrior closed on him the door of svarga, heaven.
[3] Conqueror of foes.
[4] More often translated, "desirous of wealth," but the word is used elsewhere for well-wisher, "desirous of good," and the term is more in accordance with the tone of Arjuna's remarks.
[5] Dharma.

Gudâkesha, conqueror of his foes, having thus addressed Hrishîkesha and said to Govinda, "I will not fight!", became silent.(9)

Then Hrishîkesha, smiling, as it were, O Bhârata, spake these words to him, despondent, in the midst of the two armies:(10)

The Blessed Lord said:

Thou grievest for those that should not be grieved for, yet speakest words of wisdom.[6] The wise grieve neither for the living nor for the dead.(11)

Nor at any time verily was I not, nor thou, nor these princes of men, nor verily shall we ever cease to be, hereafter.(12)

As the dweller in the body experienceth in the body childhood, youth, old age, so passeth he on to another body; the steadfast one grieveth not thereat.(13)

The contacts of matter, O son of Kuntî, giving cold and heat, pleasure and pain, they come and go, impermanent; endure them bravely, O Bhârata.(14)

The man whom these torment not, O chief of men, balanced in pain and pleasure, steadfast, he is fitted for immortality.(15)

The unreal hath no being; the real never ceaseth to be; the truth about both hath been perceived by the seers of the essence of things.[7] (16)

Know That to be indestructible by whom all this is pervaded. Nor can any work the destruction of that imperishable One.(17)

These bodies of the embodied One, who is eternal, indestructible and immeasurable, are known as finite. Therefore fight, O Bhârata.(18)

He who regardeth this[8] as a slayer, and he who thinketh he is slain, both of them are ignorant. He slayeth not, nor is he slain.(19)

He is not born, nor doth he die; nor having been, ceaseth he any more to be; unborn, perpetual, eternal and ancient, he is not slain when the body is slaughtered.(20)

---

[6] Words that sound wise, but miss the deeper sense of wisdom.
[7] Tattva.
[8] The dweller in the body.

Who knoweth him indestructible, perpetual, unborn, undiminishing, how can that man slay, O Pârtha, or cause to be slain?(21)

As a man, casting off worn-out garments, taketh new ones, so the dweller in the body, casting off worn-out bodies, entereth into others that are new.(22)

Weapons cleave him not, nor fire burneth him, nor waters wet him, nor wind drieth him away.(23)

Uncleavable he, incombustible he, and indeed neither to be wetted nor dried away; perpetual, all-pervasive, stable, immovable, ancient.(24)

Unmanifest, unthinkable, immutable, he is called; therefore knowing him as such, thou shouldst not grieve.(25)

Or if thou thinkest of him as being constantly born and constantly dying, even then, O mighty-armed, thou shouldst not grieve.(26)

For certain is death for the born, and certain is birth for the dead; therefore over the inevitable thou shouldst not grieve.(27)

Beings are unmanifest in their origin, manifest in their midmost state, O Bhârata, unmanifest likewise are they in dissolution. What room then for lamentation?(28)

As marvellous one regardeth him; as marvellous another speaketh thereof; as marvellous another heareth thereof; yet having heard none indeed understandeth.(29)

This dweller in the body of everyone is ever invulnerable, O Bhârata; therefore thou shouldst not grieve for any creature.(30)

Further, looking to thine own duty[9] thou shouldst not tremble; for there is nothing more welcome to a Kshattriya[10] than righteous war.(31)

Happy the Kshattriyas, O Pârtha, who obtain such a fight, offered unsought as an open door to heaven.(32)

---

[9] Dharma.
[10] A person of the second, the warrior, caste.

But if thou wilt not carry on this righteous warfare, then casting away thine own duty[11] and thine honour, thou wilt incur sin.(33)

Men will recount thy perpetual dishonour, and, to one highly esteemed, dishonour exceedeth death.(34)

The great car-warriors[12] will think thee fled from the battle from fear, and thou, that wast highly thought of by them, wilt be lightly held.(35)

Many unseemly words will be spoken by thine enemies, slandering thy strength; what more painful than that?(36)

Slain, thou wilt obtain heaven; victorious, thou wilt enjoy the earth; therefore stand up, O son of Kuntî, resolute to fight.(37)

Taking as equal pleasure and pain, gain and loss, victory and defeat, gird thee for the battle; thus thou shalt not incur sin.(38)

This teaching set forth to thee is in accordance with the Sânkhya[13]; hear it now according to the Yoga[14], imbued with which teaching, O Pârtha, thou shalt cast away the bonds of action.(39)

In this there is no loss of effort, nor is there transgression. Even a little of this knowledge[15] protects from great fear.(40)

The determinate Reason[16] is but one-pointed, O joy of the Kurus; many-branched and endless are the thoughts of the irresolute.(41)

Flowery speech is uttered by the foolish, rejoicing in the letter of the Vedas,[17] O Pârtha, saying: "There is naught but this";(42)

With desire for self[18], with heaven for goal, they offer birth as the fruit of action, and prescribe many and various ceremonies for the attainment of pleasure and lordship.(43)

---

[11] Dharma.
[12] The generals.
[13] One of the six systems of Indian philosophy dealing with evolution.
[14] Another of the same systems, dealing with meditation.
[15] Dharma.
[16] Buddhi.
[17] The Hindu Scriptures.
[18] Those whose very self is desire, Kâma, and who therefore act with a view to win heaven and also rebirth to wealth and rank.

For them who cling to pleasure and lordship, whose minds are captivated by such teaching, is not designed this determinate Reason,[19] on contemplation[20] steadily bent.[21] (44)

The Vedas deal with the three attributes[22]; be thou above these three attributes, O Arjuna; beyond the pairs of opposites, ever steadfast in purity,[23] careless of possessions, full of the Self.(45)

All the Vedas are as useful to an enlightened Brâhmana[24] as is a tank in a place covered all over with water.(46)

Thy business is with the action only, never with its fruits; so let not the fruit of action be thy motive, nor be thou to inaction attached.(47)

Perform action, O Dhananjaya, dwelling in union with the divine,[25] renouncing attachments and balanced evenly in success and failure: equilibrium is called yoga.(48)

Far lower than the Yoga of Discrimination[26] is action, O Dhananjaya. Take thou refuge in the Pure Reason[27]; pitiable are they who work for fruit.(49)

United to the Pure Reason[27] one abandoneth here both good and evil deeds; therefore cleave thou to yoga; yoga is skill in action.(50)

---

[19] Buddhi.

[20] Samadhi, the third state of consciousness in meditation.

[21] The following alternative translation of Slokas 42, 43, and 44 is offered: "The flowery speech that the unwise utter, O Pârtha, clinging to the word of the Veda, saying there is nothing else, ensouled by desire and longing after heaven, (the speech) that offereth only rebirth as the (ultimate) fruit of action, that is full of (recommendations to) various rites for the sake of (gaining) enjoyments and sovereignty—the thought of those misled by that (speech), cleaving to pleasures and lordship, not being inspired with resolution, is not engaged in contemplation." This is closer to the original, which is all in one sentence.

[22] Gunas = attributes, or forms of energy. They are sattva, rhythm, harmony, or purity; rajas, motion, activity, or passion; tamas, inertia, darkness, or stupidity.

[23] Sattva.

[24] A person of the highest, the priestly and teaching caste.

[25] Dwelling in yoga, union.

[26] Union with Buddhi, the innermost sheath (or vehicle) of Atma.

[27] Buddhi.

The Sages, united to the Pure Reason[27], renounce the fruit which action yieldeth, and, liberated from the bonds of birth, they go to the blissful seat.(51)

When thy mind[28] shall escape from this tangle of delusion, then thou shalt rise to indifference as to what has been heard and shall be heard.(52)

When thy mind[28], bewildered by the Scriptures[29], shall stand immovable, fixed in contemplation, then shalt thou attain unto yoga[30].(53)

Arjuna said:

What the mark, of him who is stable of mind,[31] steadfast in contemplation, O Keshava? How doth the stable-minded[32] talk, how doth he sit, how walk?(54)

The Blessed Lord said:

When a man abandoneth, O Pârtha, all the desires of the heart[33], and is satisfied in the Self by the Self, then is he called stable in mind[34].(55)

He whose mind[34] is free from anxiety amid pains, indifferent amid pleasures, loosed from passion, fear and anger, is called a sage[35] of stable mind.[36] (56)

He who on every side is without attachments, whatever hap of fair and foul, who neither likes nor dislikes, of such a one the understanding[37] is well poised.(57)

---

[28] Buddhi.

[29] Sruti.

[30] To union with Atma, the Self; yoga implies harmony with the divine will. The word translated contemplation is, as before, Samâdhi.

[31] Prajnâ.

[32] Dhî.

[33] Manah.

[34] Prajnâ.

[35] A Muni, *i.e.*, a saint or ascetic: in its original meaning, one who observed the vow of silence.

[36] Dhî.

[37] Prajnâ.

When, again, as a tortoise draws in on all sides its limbs, he withdraws his senses from the objects of sense, then is his understanding[37] well poised.(58)

The objects of sense, but not the relish for them,[38] turn away from an abstemious dweller in the body; and even relish turneth away from him after the Supreme is seen.(59)

O son of Kuntî, the excited senses of even a wise man, though he be striving, impetuously carry away his mind[39].(60)

Having restrained them all, he should sit harmonised, I his supreme goal; for, whose senses are mastered, of him the understanding[40] is well poised.(61)

Man, musing on the objects of sense, conceiveth an attachment to these; from attachment ariseth desire; from desire anger[41] cometh forth;(62)

From anger proceedeth delusion; from delusion confused memory; from confused memory the destruction of Reason[42]; from destruction of Reason he perishes.(63)

But the disciplined self, moving among sense-objects with senses free from attraction and repulsion, mastered by the Self, goeth to peace.(64)

In that Peace the extinction of all pains ariseth for him, for of him whose heart[43] is peaceful the Reason[44] soon attaineth equilibrium.(65)

There is no Pure Reason for the non-harmonised, nor for the non-harmonised is there concentration[45]; for him without concentration there is no peace, and for the unpeaceful how can there be happiness?(66)

---

[38] The objects turn away when rejected, but still desire for them remains; even desire is lost when the Supreme is seen.
[39] Manah.
[40] Prajnâ.
[41] Krodha.
[42] Buddhi here implying specially Discrimination.
[43] Chetah.
[44] Buddhi.
[45] Bhâvanâ.

Such of the roving senses as the mind[46] yieldeth to, that hurries away the understanding[47], just as the gale hurries away a ship upon the waters.(67)

Therefore, O mighty-armed, whose senses are all completely restrained from the objects of sense, of him the understanding is well poised.(68)

That which is the night of all beings, for the disciplined man is the time of waking; when other beings are waking, then is it night for the sage who seeth[48].(69)

He attaineth Peace, into whom all desires flow as rivers flow into the ocean, which is filled with water, but remaineth unmoved—not he who desireth desires.(70)

Whoso forsaketh all desires and goeth onwards free from yearnings, selfless and without egoism—he goeth to Peace.(71)

This is the Eternal state, O son of Prithâ. Having attained thereto, none is bewildered. Who, even at the death-hour, is established therein, he goeth to the Nirvâna of the Eternal.(72)

Thus in the glorious Upanishads of the Bhagavad-Gita, the science of the Eternal, the scripture of Yoga, the dialogue between Sri Krishna and Arjuna, the second discourse, entitled:

YOGA BY THE SANKHYA.

---

[46] Manah.

[47] Prajnâ.

[48] The sage is awake to things over which the ordinary man sleeps and the eyes of the sage are open to truths shut out from the common vision, while *vice versa* that which is real for the masses is illusion for the sage.

THIRD DISCOURSE

The Path of Action

Chapter 3 of the *Bhagavad Gita*, known as *Karma Yoga* (The Yoga of Selfless Action), builds upon the foundational teachings of Chapter 2. Here, Arjuna, still grappling with Krishna's instruction, raises an important question: If knowledge (*Jnana Yoga*) is superior to action, why should he engage in battle at all? Krishna responds by explaining that action is necessary, but it must be performed with detachment and selflessness.

This chapter emphasizes that no one can truly renounce action. Even the act of living itself is an engagement with the world. Instead of abandoning responsibility, Krishna urges Arjuna to cultivate selfless action (Nishkama Karma), acting without attachment to rewards. Through this teaching, Krishna introduces one of the most profound principles of the *Bhagavad Gita*: the path to liberation is not through inaction, but through performing one's duty with a pure mind and without selfish motives.

The Inescapability of Action

Krishna makes it clear that renouncing action is impossible. Every living being is bound by Prakriti (Nature) and must act according to its inherent qualities. Even those who seek spiritual wisdom must still engage with the world. True renunciation is not about abandoning responsibilities but performing them with detachment.

Krishna presents the example of great sages and leaders—they do not withdraw from the world but instead lead by example, performing their duties with discipline and selflessness. If they were to cease acting, society would descend into chaos. Similarly, Arjuna, as a warrior, must fight—not for personal gain, but because it is his duty (Dharma).

Karma Yoga: The Art of Selfless Action

The heart of this chapter revolves around Karma Yoga, the discipline of action without attachment. Krishna advises Arjuna to perform his duty while renouncing attachment to the fruits of his labor. He teaches that when actions are performed as an offering to the divine, rather than for personal benefit, they become a means of spiritual liberation. This

28

detachment transforms work into a form of worship, allowing the individual to remain balanced in both success and failure.

Krishna contrasts selfish action, which binds one to the cycle of rebirth, with selfless action, which purifies the soul. Those who act without desire for personal gain achieve freedom, while those who act out of greed, attachment, or ego remain trapped in suffering.

The Importance of Duty (Svadharma)

One of the key teachings of Chapter 3 is the importance of Svadharma (one's personal duty). Krishna reminds Arjuna that it is better to perform one's own duty imperfectly than to take on another's duty, even if done perfectly. Each individual has a role to play in the cosmic order, and attempting to escape this role leads only to confusion and inner conflict.

This teaching reinforces the idea that life itself is structured around responsibility and discipline. One cannot abandon action simply because it is difficult or unpleasant. Instead, embracing duty with a sense of service leads to inner peace.

The Influence of Gunas (Modes of Nature)

Krishna introduces the concept of the three Gunas (qualities of nature)— Sattva (purity and wisdom), Rajas (passion and activity), and Tamas (inertia and ignorance). These govern human tendencies and behaviors, influencing how we act and respond to situations. Understanding these forces helps one cultivate self-awareness and move toward higher consciousness.

Those dominated by Rajas (passion and desire) are attached to results, always chasing success and fearing failure. Those influenced by Tamas (ignorance and lethargy) avoid action altogether, leading to stagnation and delusion. The ideal state, according to Krishna, is to act with the clarity of Sattva, performing duties selflessly and without personal attachment.

Krishna's Final Advice: Lead by Example

Krishna explains that wise individuals must act not for themselves, but for the welfare of others. By performing duties without ego or selfishness, they set an example for the world. Leaders, teachers, and spiritual seekers all bear responsibility for guiding others, and they must do so through action, not mere words.

He also warns Arjuna against becoming enslaved by personal desires, urging him to dedicate all actions to the divine. By aligning oneself with a higher purpose, one can transcend suffering and attain true peace.

The Call to Action

Chapter 3 is a call to engagement with the world, rather than withdrawal. Krishna dismantles the illusion that wisdom means abandoning one's duties; instead, he asserts that true wisdom lies in performing one's role with selflessness and devotion.

For Arjuna, this means embracing his duty as a warrior, not out of personal ambition, but as an offering to a higher order. For spiritual seekers, this chapter serves as a reminder that work, when done in the right spirit, becomes a tool for liberation.

As the dialogue progresses, Krishna will introduce even deeper spiritual insights, leading Arjuna toward a more profound understanding of devotion, knowledge, and self-realization. But before one can seek liberation, one must first master the art of selfless action.

———————

Arjuna said:

If it be thought by Thee that knowledge is superior to action, O Janârdana, why dost Thou, O Keshava, enjoin on me this terrible action?(1)

With these perplexing words Thou only confusest my understanding[1]; therefore tell me with certainty the one way by which I may reach bliss.(2)

The Blessed Lord said:

In this world there is a twofold path, as I before said, O sinless one: that of yoga by knowledge, of the Sânkhyas; and that of yoga by action, of the Yogis.(3)

Man winneth not freedom from action by abstaining from activity, nor by mere renunciation doth he rise to perfection.(4)

———————

[1] Buddhi.

Nor can anyone, even for an instant, remain really actionless; for helplessly is everyone driven to action by the qualities[2] born of nature[3].(5)

Who sitteth, controlling the organs of action, but dwelling in his mind[4] on the objects of the senses, that bewildered man is called a hypocrite.(6)

But who, controlling the senses by the mind[4], O Arjuna, with the organs of action without attachment, performeth yoga by action[5], he is worthy.(7)

Perform thou right[6] action, for, action is superior to inaction, and, inactive, even the maintenance of thy body would not be possible.(8)

The world is bound by action, unless performed for the sake of sacrifice; for that sake, free from attachment, O son of Kuntî, perform thou action.(9)

Having in ancient times emanated mankind together with sacrifice, the Lord of emanation[7] said: "By this shall ye propagate; be this to you the giver of desire[8];(10)

"With this nourish ye the Shining Ones, and may the Shining Ones nourish you; thus nourishing one another ye shall reap the supremest good.(11)

"For, nourished by sacrifice, the Shining Ones shall bestow on you the enjoyments you desire." A thief verily is he who enjoyeth what is given by Them without returning Them aught.(12)

The righteous, who eat the remains of the sacrifice, are freed from all sins; but the impious, who dress food for their own sakes, they verily eat sin.(13)

From food creatures become; from rain is the production of food; rain proceedeth from sacrifice; sacrifice ariseth out of action.(14)

---

[2] Gunas.
[3] Prakriti.
[4] Manah.
[5] Karma-Yoga is the consecration of physical energy on the divine Altar; *i.e.*, the using of one's organs of action simply in service, in obedience to Law and Duty.
[6] Regulated, prescribed as a duty; or, regularly.
[7] Prajâpati.
[8] Kâmadhuk, the cow of Indra, from which each could milk what he wished for; hence the giver of desired objects.

Know thou that from Brahma[9] action groweth, and Brahma from the Imperishable cometh. Therefore the Eternal, the all-permeating, is ever present in sacrifice.(15)

He who on earth doth not follow the wheel thus revolving, sinful of life and rejoicing in the senses, he, O son of Pritha, liveth in vain.(16)

But the man who rejoiceth in the Self, with the Self is satisfied, and is content in the Self, for him verily there is nothing to do;(17)

For him there is no interest in things done, in this world, nor any in things not done, nor doth any object of his depend on any being.(18)

Therefore, without attachment, constantly perform action which is duty, for, by performing action without attachment, man verily reacheth the Supreme.(19)

Janaka and others indeed attained to perfection by action: then having an eye to the welfare of he world also, thou shouldst perform action.(20)

Whatsoever a great man doeth, that other men also do; the standard he setteth up, by that the people go.(21)

There is nothing in the three worlds, O Pârtha, that should be done by Me, nor anything unattained that might be attained; yet I mingle in action.(22)

For if I mingled not ever in action unwearied, men all around would follow My path, O son of Prithâ.(23)

These worlds would fall into ruin, if I did not perform action; I should be the author of confusion of castes, and should destroy these creatures.(24)

As the ignorant act from attachment to action, O Bhârata, so should the wise act without attachment, desiring the welfare of the world.(25)

Let no wise man unsettle the mind of ignorant people attached to action; but acting in harmony with Me let him render all action attractive.(26)

All actions are wrought by the qualities[10] of nature only. The self, deluded by egoism[11], thinketh: "I am the doer."(27)

---

[9] An Indian of much knowledge translates Brahma here as "the Vedas."
[10] Gunas.
[11] Ahamkâra, the separate "I am."

But he, O mighty-armed, who knoweth the essence of the divisions of the qualities and functions, holding that "the qualities move amid the qualities,"[12] is not attached.(28)

Those deluded by the qualities of nature are attached to the functions of the qualities. The man of perfect knowledge should not unsettle the foolish whose knowledge is imperfect.(29)

Surrendering all actions to Me, with thy thoughts resting on the supreme Self, from hope and egoism freed, and of mental fever cured, engage in battle.(30)

Who abide ever in this teaching of Mine full of faith and free from caviling, they too are released from actions.(31)

Who carp at My teaching and act not thereon, senseless, deluded in all knowledge, know thou these mindless ones as fated to be destroyed.(32)

Even the man of knowledge behaves in conformity with his own nature; beings follow nature; what shall restraint avail?(33)

Affection and aversion for the objects of sense abide in the senses; let none come under the dominion of these two; they are obstructors of the path.(34)

Better one's own duty,[13] though destitute of merit, than the duty[13] of another, well discharged. Better death in the discharge of one's own duty;[13] the duty[13] of another is full of danger.(35)

Arjuna said:

But dragged on by what does a man commit sin, reluctantly indeed, O Varshneya, as it were by force constrained?(36)

The Blessed Lord said:

---

[12] The Gunas, qualities, as sense-organs move amid the Gunas, qualities, as sense-objects. A suggested reading is "The functions dwell in the propensities." Sankarâchârya says, "of the class of qualities and the class of actions;" or the arrangement, or relations of qualities and actions.
[13] Dharma.

It is desire, it is wrath, begotten by the quality of motion[14]; all-consuming, all-polluting, know thou this as our foe here on earth.(37)

As a flame is enveloped by smoke, as a mirror by dust, as an embryo is wrapped by the amnion, so This[15] is enveloped by it.(38)

Enveloped is wisdom by this constant enemy of the wise in the form of desire, which is insatiable as a flame.(39)

The senses, the mind[16] and the Reason[17] are said to be its seat; by these enveloping wisdom, it bewilders the dweller in the body.(40)

Therefore, O best of the Bhâratas, mastering first the senses, do thou slay this thing of sin, destructive of wisdom and knowledge.(41)

It is said that the senses are great; greater than the senses is the mind:[16] greater than the mind[16] is the Reason;[17] but what is greater than the Reason,[17] is He[18].(42

Thus understanding Him as greater than the Reason,[19] restraining the self by the Self, slay thou, O mighty-armed, the enemy in the form of desire, difficult to overcome.(43)

Thus in the glorious Upanishads of the Bhagavad-Gita, the science of the Eternal, the scripture of Yoga, the dialogue between Sri Krishna and Arjuna, the third discourse, entitled:

THE YOGA OF ACTION.

---

[14] Rajah.

[15] The universe: "This" as opposed to "That" the Eternal. Some say "This" stands for knowledge.

[16] Manah.

[17] Buddhi.

[18] The Supreme.

[19] Buddhi.

FOURTH DISCOURSE

The Divine Origin of Knowledge

In Chapter 4 of the *Bhagavad Gita*, known as *Jnana Karma Sannyasa Yoga* (The Yoga of Knowledge and Renunciation of Action), Krishna expands upon the teachings of *Karma Yoga* from the previous chapter. He explains that **true knowledge (Jnana)** is essential for liberation and that all actions must be performed with wisdom and detachment. This chapter also reveals Krishna's divine nature, marking a turning point in the dialogue. Here, Krishna explains the eternal transmission of wisdom and the importance of performing action without attachment, reinforcing the principles of selfless service.

At the outset, Krishna reveals that he has taught this sacred knowledge since time immemorial, passing it down through generations of sages and kings. Arjuna, confused by this statement, questions how Krishna could have existed before these ancient teachers. In response, Krishna unveils his divine reality—he is not merely Arjuna's charioteer but the eternal and cosmic manifestation of the Divine. This revelation elevates the *Bhagavad Gita* beyond a simple philosophical discourse, embedding it within the realm of divine revelation and universal truth.

Krishna's Divine Incarnation and Cosmic Mission

One of the most profound teachings in this chapter is Krishna's declaration that whenever dharma declines and adharma (unrighteousness) rises, he manifests himself on Earth to restore balance. This concept of divine incarnation (avatar) is fundamental to Hinduism—Krishna asserts that he has been and will continue to be born in various forms to guide humanity toward righteousness.

This teaching reassures Arjuna that the war he faces is not just a personal or political struggle but part of a greater cosmic order. Krishna's presence on the battlefield is not arbitrary; he has taken form to uphold dharma and protect righteousness. This revelation provides Arjuna with a broader perspective, helping him move beyond his personal doubts and align himself with a divine purpose.

The Power of Selfless Sacrifice

Krishna further elaborates on the principle of **Yajna (sacrifice)**—a concept that extends beyond ritual offerings into the very philosophy of selfless action. He explains that all actions, when performed as an offering to the divine rather than for personal gain, become a sacred act. This purifies the soul and frees one from karmic bondage.

The various types of sacrifices described in this chapter are not just external rituals but also inner disciplines—offering knowledge, devotion, and service as a means of connecting with the divine. Krishna highlights that those who act with wisdom, dedicating their work as a sacrifice to the greater good, attain liberation.

The Path of Knowledge (Jnana Yoga)

Krishna then distinguishes between mere action and action rooted in wisdom. He explains that knowledge is the highest form of purification—true wisdom burns away ignorance just as fire consumes fuel. Unlike action performed in ignorance, action grounded in knowledge leads to liberation.

Arjuna is encouraged to seek wisdom from enlightened beings, approaching them with humility and devotion. Krishna emphasizes that knowledge must be received through a proper teacher (Guru) and absorbed with an open heart. Only through knowledge can one **see beyond illusion (Maya) and recognize the eternal self (Atman).**

Renunciation of Action Through Wisdom

Krishna redefines the meaning of renunciation (*Sannyasa*), teaching that true renunciation is not the abandonment of action but the abandonment of attachment to results. The enlightened being performs actions without being bound by them, moving through life as a lotus remains untouched by the water it floats upon.

This insight bridges the paths of **Karma Yoga (selfless action) and Jnana Yoga (wisdom)**—one does not need to renounce the world to attain liberation. Instead, one must act with wisdom and detachment, seeing all actions as part of the divine plan. Through this, Krishna resolves the tension between engagement with the world and spiritual transcendence, teaching that both can coexist harmoniously.

The Call to Act with Wisdom

Krishna concludes this chapter by urging Arjuna to embrace wisdom and action together. He reassures Arjuna that once he attains knowledge, all his doubts will dissolve, and he will act with clarity, conviction, and devotion. Krishna's message is clear: action performed with knowledge and detachment leads to freedom, while ignorance leads to bondage.

With this understanding, Arjuna is now equipped with a broader spiritual vision—he no longer fights merely as a warrior but as an instrument of divine will. This chapter prepares him for the deeper teachings that will follow, where Krishna will further elaborate on devotion, surrender, and the ultimate nature of reality.

Thus, the fourth discourse of the *Bhagavad Gita* teaches that wisdom and action must go hand in hand. True renunciation is not withdrawal from the world but acting with complete surrender and understanding. It is in this balance that one finds ultimate liberation.

The Blessed Lord said:

This imperishable yoga I declared to Vivasvân; Vivasvân taught it to Manu; Manu to Ikshvâku told it.(1)

This, handed on down the line, the King-Sages knew. This yoga by great efflux of time decayed in the world, O Parantapa.(2)

This same ancient yoga hath been to-day declared to thee by Me, for thou art My devotee and My friend; it is the supreme Secret.(3)

Arjuna said:

Later was Thy birth, earlier the birth of Vivasvân; how then am I to understand that Thou declaredst it in the beginning?(4)

The Blessed Lord said:

Many births have been left behind by Me and by thee, O Arjuna. I know them all, but thou knowest not thine, O Parantapa.(5)

Though unborn, the imperishable Self, and also the Lord of all beings, brooding over nature which is Mine own, yet I am born through My own Power.[1] (6)

Whenever there is decay of righteousness,[2] O Bhârata, and there is exaltation of unrighteousness,[3] then I Myself come forth;(7)

For the protection of the good, for the destruction of evil-doers, for the sake of firmly establishing righteousness[2], I am born from age to age.(8)

He who thus knoweth My divine birth and action, in its essence, having abandoned the body, cometh not to birth again, but cometh unto Me, O Arjuna.(9)

Freed from passion, fear and anger, filled with Me, taking refuge in Me, purified in the fire[4] of wisdom, many have entered into My Being.(10)

However men approach Me, even so do I welcome them, for the path men take from every side is Mine, O Pârtha.(11)

They who long after success in action on earth worship the Shining Ones; for in brief space verily, in this world of men, success is born of action.(12)

The four castes were emanated by Me, by the different distribution of qualities[5] and actions; know Me to be the author of them, though the actionless and inexhaustible.(13)

Nor do actions affect Me, nor is the fruit of action desired by Me. He who thus knoweth Me is not bound by actions.(14)

Having thus known, our forefathers, ever seeking liberation, performed action; therefore do thou also perform action, as did our forefathers in the olden time.(15)

---

[1] Mâyâ, the power of thought that produces form, which is transient and therefore unreal compared with the eternal Reality; hence Mâyâ comes to be taken as the power of producing illusion.
[2] Dharma.
[3] Adharma, the opposite of dharma, all that is disorderly, against the nature of things.
[4] Tapas, from tap, blazing like fire.
[5] Gunas.

"What is action, what inaction"? Even the wise are herein perplexed. Therefore I will declare to thee the action by knowing which thou shalt be loosed from evil.(16)

It is needful to discriminate action, to discriminate unlawful action, and to discriminate inaction; mysterious is the path of action.(17)

He who seeth inaction in action, and action in inaction, he is wise among men, he is harmonious, even while performing all action.(18)

Whose works are all free from the moulding of desire, whose actions are burned up by the fire of wisdom, him the wise have called a Sage.(19)

Having abandoned attachment to the fruit of action, always content, nowhere seeking refuge, he is not doing anything, although doing actions.(20)

Hoping for naught, his mind and self controlled, having abandoned all greed, performing action by the body alone, he doth not commit sin.(21)

Content with whatsoever he obtaineth without effort, free from the pairs of opposites, without envy, balanced in success and failure, though acting he is not bound.(22)

Of one with attachment dead, harmonious, with his thoughts established in wisdom, his works sacrifices, all action melts away.(23)

The Eternal the oblation, the Eternal the clarified butter, are offered in the Eternal the fire by the Eternal; unto the Eternal verily shall he go who in his action meditateth wholly upon the Eternal.[6] (24)

Some Yogis offer up sacrifice to the Shining Ones[7]; others sacrifice only by pouring sacrifice into the fire of the Eternal;(25)

Some pour as sacrifice hearing and the other senses into the fires of restraint; some pour sound and the other objects of sense into the fires of the senses as sacrifice;(26)

Others again into the wisdom-kindled fire of union attained by self-control, pour as sacrifice all the functions of the senses and the functions of life;(27)

---

[6] He who sees the Eternal beneath the transitory alone goes to the Eternal; all others remain bound in the world of forms.
[7] Literally, divine sacrifice.

Yet others the sacrifice of wealth, the sacrifice of austerity, the sacrifice of yoga, the sacrifice of silent reading and wisdom, men concentrated and of effectual vows;(28)

Yet others pour as sacrifice the outgoing breath in the incoming, and the incoming in the outgoing, restraining the flow of the outgoing and incoming breaths, solely absorbed in the control of breathing.[8] (29)

Others regular in food, pour as sacrifice their life-breaths in life-breaths. All these are knowers of sacrifice, and by sacrifice have destroyed their sins.(30)

The eaters of the life-giving[9] remains of sacrifice go to the changeless Eternal. This world is not for the non-sacrificer, much less the other, O best of the Kurus.(31)

Many and various sacrifices are thus spread out before the Eternal.[10] Know thou that all these are born of action, and thus knowing thou shalt be free.(32)

Better than the sacrifice of any objects is the sacrifice of wisdom, O Parantapa. All actions in their entirety, O Pârtha, culminate in wisdom.(33)

Learn thou this by discipleship,[11] by investigation, and by service. The wise, the seers of the essence of things, will instruct thee in wisdom.(34)

And having known this, thou shalt not again fall into this confusion, O Pândava; for by this thou wilt see all beings without exception in the Self, and thus in Me.(35)

Even if thou art the most sinful of all sinners, yet shalt thou cross over all sin by the raft of wisdom.(36)

As the burning fire reduces fuel to ashes, O Arjuna, so doth the fire of wisdom reduce all actions to ashes.(37)

---

[8] Prânâyâma, restraint of breath, a technical name for this practice.

[9] Amrita: it is the elixir of immortality, and the amrita-remains, therefore, are foods that give immortality.

[10] "In the Vedas" is another interpretation.

[11] Literally, falling at the feet, *i.e.*, the feet of the teacher.

Verily there is no purifier in this world like wisdom; he that is perfected in yoga finds it in the Self in due season.(38)

The man who is full of faith[12] obtaineth wisdom, and he also who hath mastery over his senses; and, having obtained wisdom, he goeth swiftly to the supreme Peace.(39)

But the ignorant, faithless, doubting self goeth to destruction; nor this world, nor that beyond, nor happiness, is there for the doubting self.(40)

He who hath renounced actions by yoga, who hath cloven asunder doubt by wisdom, who is ruled by the Self,[13] actions do not bind him, O Dhananjaya.(41)

Therefore, with the sword of the wisdom of the Self cleaving asunder this ignorance-born doubt dwelling in thy heart, be established in yoga. Stand up, O Bhârata.(42)

Thus in the glorious Upanishads of the Bhagavad-Gita, the science of the Eternal, the scripture of Yoga the dialogue between Shri Krishna and Arjuna, the fourth discourse, entitled:

THE YOGA OF WISDOM.

---

[12] Who is intent upon faith.
[13] Madhusûdana explains *âtmavantam* as "always watchful."

FIFTH DISCOURSE

The Path of Renunciation and Action

In Chapter 5 of the *Bhagavad Gita*, known as *Karma Sannyasa Yoga* (The Yoga of Renunciation and Selfless Action), Krishna continues his discourse on the relationship between renunciation (sannyasa) and action (karma yoga). Arjuna, still seeking clarity, asks Krishna to definitively state which path is superior—renouncing the world or remaining engaged in action. Krishna answers that both paths can lead to liberation, but the path of selfless action is superior for most seekers.

Krishna explains that true renunciation is not about physical withdrawal from the world but about mentally detaching from the fruits of one's actions. A true renunciate is one who performs duties without selfish motives, dedicating all work to the divine. Thus, **Karma Yoga (selfless action) and Sannyasa (renunciation)** are ultimately one and the same when performed with the right understanding.

True Renunciation: A Mental State, Not Mere Inaction

Krishna emphasizes that **renunciation does not mean abandoning action altogether**. Those who seek liberation by renouncing responsibilities without inner detachment are merely avoiding their dharma. The real *sannyasi* is not one who rejects work but one who remains active while renouncing personal attachment to the results.

He makes it clear that those who act without desire or personal gain experience inner peace, while those who act out of selfish motives remain bound by karma. The key distinction lies in how one approaches work—if done in a spirit of surrender and detachment, even worldly activities become a means of spiritual liberation.

Equanimity: The Mark of a True Yogi

A major theme in this chapter is **equanimity (samatva)**—the ability to remain unaffected by pleasure and pain, success and failure, praise and criticism. Krishna teaches that one who sees all experiences with an equal mind has attained true wisdom. Such a person understands that the fluctuations of life are temporary and that the eternal self remains untouched by external circumstances.

This quality of equanimity is essential to spiritual growth. Krishna reminds Arjuna that liberation is not dependent on outward conditions but on inner stability. A person who remains calm and undisturbed in all situations naturally moves toward liberation.

Seeing the Divine in All Beings

Krishna introduces the concept of spiritual vision—the ability to see beyond physical appearances and recognize the same divine presence in all beings. The enlightened person does not distinguish between the wise scholar, the humble servant, the nobleman, or even the lowest outcast. Instead, they see all beings as manifestations of the **same eternal consciousness (Atman).**

This teaching reinforces the idea that spiritual progress is not about status, wealth, or ritualistic practices but about perception and awareness. By cultivating this vision, one moves beyond prejudice, ego, and attachment, leading to a state of oneness with the universe.

Liberation Through Detachment and Devotion

Krishna reassures Arjuna that true freedom is attained by realizing one's inner divinity and acting with detachment. He explains that a person who dedicates all actions to the divine, free from attachment, neither rejoices in success nor grieves in failure. Such a person transcends the dualities of the world and attains **Brahmanirvana—the state of merging with the Supreme**.

By surrendering to the divine and working without selfish motives, the seeker experiences inner peace and joy beyond material pleasure. Krishna describes this state as one of deep inner satisfaction, where the soul is content within itself, free from external dependencies.

The Path to Ultimate Peace

Krishna concludes this chapter by emphasizing that peace comes from surrendering personal ego and acting in harmony with the divine will. Those who remain caught in personal desires and attachments remain restless, while those who relinquish self-centered ambitions attain true contentment. He urges Arjuna to act without pride, anger, or desire, dedicating all actions to the divine.

In this teaching, Krishna bridges Karma Yoga (the path of action) and Jnana Yoga (the path of knowledge), showing that selfless action performed with wisdom leads to the highest spiritual realization.

The Union of Knowledge and Action

Chapter 5 serves as a synthesis of the teachings from the previous chapters. Krishna dismantles the misconception that renunciation and action are opposing paths, instead revealing that both are equally valid when performed with detachment and wisdom.

For Arjuna, this chapter further clarifies that his duty as a warrior is not an obstacle to liberation but a means to attain it. By fulfilling his dharma with selflessness, he aligns himself with the divine order. For spiritual seekers, the message is clear: it is not external renunciation that leads to freedom, but the inner renunciation of attachment and ego.

This teaching prepares the ground for Krishna's next discourse, where he will introduce **the importance of devotion (Bhakti Yoga)** and how surrendering to the divine is the highest path of all. But before reaching that stage, one must first learn to act without bondage, without fear, and without selfish desire.

————————

Arjuna said:

Renunciation of actions Thou praisest, O Krishna, and then also yoga. Of the two which one is the better? That tell me conclusively.(1)

The Blessed Lord said:

Renunciation and yoga by action both lead to the highest bliss; of the two, yoga by action is verily better than renunciation of action.(2)

He should be known as a perpetual ascetic,[1] who neither hateth nor desireth; free from the pairs of opposites, O mighty-armed, he is easily set free from bondage.(3)

———————————————

[1] Sannyâsi; one who renounces all.

Children, not sages, speak of the Sânkhya and the Yoga as different; he who is duly established in one obtaineth the fruits of both.(4)

That place which is gained by the Sânkhyas is reached by the Yogîs also. He seeth, who seeth that the Sânkhya and the Yoga are one.(5)

But without yoga, O mighty-armed, renunciation is hard to attain to; the yoga-harmonised Muni swiftly goeth to the Eternal.(6)

He who is harmonised by yoga, the self purified, Self-ruled, the senses subdued, whose Self is the Self of all beings, although acting he is not affected.(7)

"I do not anything," should think the harmonised one, who knoweth the essence of things; seeing, hearing, touching, smelling, eating, moving, sleeping, breathing.(8)

Speaking, giving, grasping, opening and closing the eyes, he holdeth: "The senses move among the objects of the senses."(9)

He who acteth, placing all actions in the Eternal, abandoning attachment, is unaffected by sin as a lotus leaf by the waters.(10)

Yogis, having abandoned attachment, perform action only by the body, by the mind[2], by the Reason[3], and even by the senses, for the purification of the self.(11)

The harmonised man, having abandoned the fruit of action, attaineth to the eternal Peace; the non-harmonised, impelled by desire, attached to fruit, are bound.(12)

Mentally renouncing all actions, the sovereign dweller in the body resteth serenely in the nine-gated city,[4] neither acting nor causing to act.(13)

The Lord of the world produceth not the idea of agency, nor actions, nor the union together of action and its fruit; nature, however, manifesteth.(14)

The Lord accepteth neither the evil-doing nor yet the well-doing of any. Wisdom is enveloped by unwisdom; therewith mortals are deluded.(15)

---

[2] Manah.
[3] Buddhi.
[4] The body, often called the city of the Eternal.

Verily, in whom unwisdom is destroyed by the wisdom of the Self, in them wisdom, shining as the sun, reveals the Supreme.(16)

Thinking on That, merged in That, established in That, solely devoted to That, they go whence there is no return, their sins dispelled by wisdom.(17)

Sages look equally on a Brâhmana adorned with learning and humility, a cow, an elephant, and even a dog and an outcaste.[5] (18)

Even here on earth everything is overcome by those whose mind[6] remains balanced; the Eternal is incorruptible and balanced; therefore they are established in the Eternal.(19)

With Reason[7] firm, unperplexed, the knower of the Eternal established in the Eternal, neither rejoiceth on obtaining what is pleasant, nor sorroweth on obtaining what is unpleasant.(20)

He, whose self is unattached to external contacts and findeth joy in the Self, having the self harmonised with the Eternal by yoga, enjoys imperishable bliss.(21)

The delights that are contact-born, they are verily wombs of pain, for they have beginning and ending, O Kaunteya; not in them may rejoice the wise.(22)

He who is able to endure here on earth, ere he be liberated from the body, the force born from desire and passion, he is harmonised, he is a happy man.(23)

He who is happy within, who rejoiceth within, who is illuminated within, that Yogî, becoming the Eternal, goeth to the Peace[8] of the Eternal.(24)

Rishis, their sins destroyed, their duality removed, their selves controlled, intent upon the welfare of all beings, obtain the Peace[8] of the Eternal.(25)

---

[5] Shvapâka, the lowest class of outcastes.
[6] Manah.
[7] Buddhi.
[8] Nirvâna.

The Peace[8] of the Eternal lies near to those who know themselves, who are disjoined from desire and passion, subdued in nature, of subdued thoughts.(26)

Having external contacts excluded, and with gaze fixed between the eyebrows; having made equal the outgoing and ingoing breaths moving within the nostrils;(27)

With senses, mind,[9] and Reason[10] ever controlled, solely pursuing liberation, the Sage, having for ever cast away desire, fear and passion, verily is liberated.(28)

Having known Me, as the Enjoyer of sacrifice and of austerity, the mighty Ruler of all the worlds, and the Lover of all beings, he goeth to Peace.(29)

Thus in the glorious Upanishads of the Bhagavad-Gita, the science of the Eternal, the scripture of Yoga, in the dialogue between Shrî Krishna and Arjuna, the fifth discourse, entitled:

THE YOGA OF THE RENUNCIATION OF ACTION.

---

[9] Manah.
[10] Buddhi.

SIXTH DISCOURSE

The Path of the Yogi

In Chapter 6 of the *Bhagavad Gita*, known as *Dhyana Yoga* (The Yoga of Meditation), Krishna expands upon the previous teachings on action and knowledge by introducing the discipline of meditation as a means to spiritual liberation. He explains that true renunciation is not about external withdrawal but about inner detachment and self-mastery.

Arjuna, still struggling with doubts, seeks clarity on how one should live to attain true wisdom. Krishna responds by outlining the qualities of a true yogi, emphasizing that meditation is the most direct path to realizing the **eternal self (Atman)** and attaining **union with the divine (Brahman).**

The True Yogi: Beyond Rituals and Renunciation

Krishna begins by distinguishing between a mere renunciate (sannyasi) and a true yogi. He explains that one does not become a yogi simply by abandoning worldly duties, nor by merely renouncing possessions. Instead, the highest yogi is one who acts selflessly, remains free from attachment, and dedicates all actions to the divine. Such a person is neither bound by work nor disturbed by inaction.

Krishna stresses that **meditation is the highest form of yoga**, superior even to asceticism, knowledge, and selfless action. The true yogi is **one who sees** all beings as equal, remains unaffected by external circumstances, and finds joy within the self.

The Discipline of Meditation (Dhyana Yoga)

Krishna outlines the practical aspects of meditation, describing how a seeker should sit, breathe, and focus the mind. He teaches that the yogi should find a quiet place, sit in a stable position, and fix the mind on the divine. The key is steadiness—the practitioner must remain unwavering in their focus, neither overindulging in the senses nor practicing extreme austerities.

By disciplining the mind and body, one transcends distractions and realizes the inner self, which is beyond birth and death. Krishna describes the state of a perfected yogi as one of deep inner peace, detached from the fluctuations of the external world. This state is attained through persistent meditation and unwavering devotion.

The Yogi's Vision: Seeing the Divine in All

One of the most profound teachings of this chapter is Krishna's assertion that **the highest yogi is the one who sees the divine in all beings**. The true yogi does not distinguish between a learned scholar, a humble servant, or even an outcast—he sees all as equal manifestations of the divine essence.

This vision of unity leads to deep compassion and selfless love. The yogi, having realized the oneness of all existence, no longer harbors desires, attachments, or fears. Instead, he moves through life with a sense of peace and universal love, serving others without ego or expectation.

The Rewards of Meditation

Krishna describes the benefits of sustained meditation, explaining that the yogi experiences true joy and freedom. Unlike material pleasures, which are fleeting, the bliss of self-realization is eternal.

Those who dedicate themselves to meditation rise above dualities such as pleasure and pain, success and failure. They experience Brahmanirvana, the state of union with the Absolute, where the soul is freed from karma and the cycle of rebirth.

Krishna reassures Arjuna that even if a yogi fails to attain liberation in this life, they will be born into a spiritually advanced family in the next. Their progress is never lost—each soul continues its journey toward enlightenment across lifetimes.

The Highest Yogi: One Who Surrenders to Krishna

Krishna concludes this discourse by declaring that among all yogis, the greatest is the one who surrenders to him with faith and devotion. While meditation leads to self-realization, **Bhakti (devotion to Krishna) is the highest path**. The yogi who meditates upon the divine with love and surrender is the most spiritually advanced.

This transition from **meditation to devotion** foreshadows the teachings of the next chapters, where Krishna will emphasize Bhakti Yoga as the ultimate means of liberation.

The Power of Meditation and Devotion

Chapter 6 teaches that meditation is not just a practice but a way of life. Krishna guides Arjuna to see that true renunciation is not escape but inner detachment, and true yoga is not just postures but deep, unwavering focus on the divine.

By disciplining the mind, cultivating inner balance, and surrendering to Krishna, one attains the highest realization—oneness with the divine. This chapter serves as a bridge between self-discipline and surrender, setting the stage for the next discourse, where Krishna will reveal **the supreme importance of love and devotion (Bhakti Yoga).**

—————

The Blessed Lord said:

He that performeth such action as his duty, independently of the fruit of action, he is an ascetic,[1] he is a Yogî, not he that is without fire, and without rites.(1)

That which is called renunciation, know thou that as yoga, O Pândava; nor doth any one become a Yogî with the formative will[2] unrenounced.(2)

For a Sage who is seeking Yoga, action is called the means; for the same Sage, when he is enthroned in yoga, serenity is called the means.(3)

When a man feeleth no attachment either for the objects of sense or for actions, renouncing the formative will,[3] then, he is said to be enthroned in yoga.(4)

Let him raise the self by the Self and not let the self become depressed; for verily is the Self the friend of the self, and also the Self the self's enemy;(5)

---

[1] The ascetic, the Sannyâsî, lights no sacrificial fire and performs no sacrifices nor ceremonies; but merely to omit these, without true renunciation, is not to be a real ascetic.
[2] Sankalpa, the imaginative faculty that makes plans for the future.
[3] Sankalpa.

The Self is the friend of the self of him in whom the self by the Self is vanquished; but to the unsubdued self[4] the Self verily becometh hostile as an enemy.(6)

The higher Self of him who is Self-controlled and peaceful is uniform in cold and heat, pleasure and pain, as well as in honour and dishonour.(7)

The Yogî[5] who is satisfied with wisdom and knowledge, unwavering,[6] whose senses are subdued, to whom a lump of earth, a stone and gold are the same, is said to be harmonised.(8)

He who regards impartially lovers, friends, and foes, strangers, neutrals, foreigners and relatives, also the righteous and unrighteous, he excelleth.(9)

Let the Yogî constantly engage himself in yoga, remaining in a secret place by himself, with thought and self subdued, free from hope and greed.(10)

In a pure place, established on a fixed seat of his own, neither very much raised nor very low, made of a cloth, a black antelope skin, and kusha grass, one over the other;(11)

There, having made the mind[7] one-pointed, with thought and the functions of the senses subdued, steady on his seat, he should practise yoga for the purification of the self.(12)

Holding the body, head and neck erect, immovably steady, looking fixedly at the point of the nose, with unseeing gaze,(13)

The self serene, fearless, firm in the vow of the Brahmachâri,[8] the mind[9] controlled, thinking on Me, harmonised, let him sit aspiring after Me.(14)

The Yogî ever united thus with the Self, with the mind[9] controlled, goeth to Peace, to the supreme Bliss[10] that abideth in Me.(15)

---

[4] Literally, the non-self.
[5] The word Yogi is used for any one who is practising yoga, as well as for the man who has attained union.
[6] Literally, rock-seated.
[7] Manah.
[8] A Brahmachârî is a man who is keeping the vow of continence, a celibate.
[9] Manah.
[10] Nirvana.

Verily yoga is not for him who eateth too much, nor who abstaineth to excess, nor who is too much addicted to sleep, nor even to wakefulness, O Arjuna.(16)

Yoga killeth out all pain for him who is regulated in eating and amusement, regulated in performing actions, regulated in sleeping and waking.(17)

When his subdued thought is fixed on the Self, free from longing after all desirable things, then it is said, "he is harmonised."(18)

As a lamp in a windless place flickereth not, to such is likened the Yogî of subdued thought, absorbed in the yoga of the Self.(19)

That in which the mind finds rest, quieted by the practice of yoga: that in which he, seeing the Self by the Self, in the Self is satisfied;(20)

That in which he findeth the supreme delight which the Reason[11] can grasp beyond the senses, wherein established he moveth not from the Reality;(21)

Which, having obtained, he thinketh there is no greater gain beyond it; wherein, established, he is not shaken even by heavy sorrow;(22)

That should be known by the name of yoga, this disconnection from the union with pain. This yoga must be clung to with a firm conviction and with undesponding mind.[12] (23)

Abandoning without reserve all desires born of the imagination,[13] by the mind[14] curbing in the aggregate of the senses on every side,(24)

Little by little let him gain tranquillity, by means of Reason[15] controlled by steadiness; having made the mind[14] abide in the Self, let him not think of anything.(25)

As often as the wavering and unsteady mind[14] goeth forth, so often reining it in, let him bring it under the control of the Self.(26)

Supreme joy is for this Yogi whose mind[14] is peaceful, whose passion-nature is calmed, who is sinless and of the nature of the Eternal.(27)

---

[11] Buddhi.
[12] Chetah.
[13] Sankalpa.
[14] Manah.
[15] Buddhi.

The Yogî who thus, ever harmonising the self, hath put away sin, he easily enjoyeth the infinite bliss of contact with the Eternal.(28)

The self, harmonised by yoga, seeth the Self abiding in all beings, all beings in the Self; everywhere he seeth the same.(29)

He who seeth Me everywhere, and seeth everything in Me, of him will I never lose hold, and he shall never lose hold of Me.(30)

He who, established in unity, worshippeth Me abiding in all beings, that Yogi liveth in Me, whatever his mode of living.(31)

He who, through the likeness of the Self[16], O Arjuna, seeth equality in everything, whether pleasant or painful, he is considered a perfect Yogî.(32)

This yoga which Thou hast declared to be by equanimity, O Madhusûdana, I see not a stable foundation for it, owing to restlessness;(33)

For the mind[17] is verily restless, O Krishna; it is impetuous, strong and difficult to bend. I deem it as hard to curb as the wind.(34)

The Blessed Lord said:

Without doubt, O mighty-armed, the mind[17] is hard to curb and restless; but it may be curbed by constant practice and by dispassion.(35)

Yoga is hard to attain, methinks, by a self that is uncontrolled; but by the Self-controlled it is attainable by properly directed energy.(36)

Arjuna said:

He who is unsubdued but who possesseth faith, with the mind[18] wandering away from yoga, failing to attain perfection in yoga, what path doth he tread, O Krishna?(37)

Fallen from both, is he destroyed like a rent cloud, unsteadfast, O mighty-armed, deluded in the path of the Eternal?(38)

Deign, O Krishna, to completely dispel this doubt of mine; for there is none to be found save Thyself able to destroy this doubt.(39)

---

[16] The same Self shining in the heart of each.
[17] Manah.
[18] Manah.

The Blessed Lord said:

O son of Prithâ, neither in this world nor in the life to come is there destruction for him; never doth any who worketh righteousness, O beloved, tread the path of woe.(40)

Having attained to the worlds of the pure-doing, and having dwelt there for immemorial years, he who fell from yoga is reborn in a pure and blessed house;(41)

Or he may even be born into a family of wise Yogîs; but such a birth as that is most difficult to obtain in this world.(42)

There he recovereth the characteristics belonging to this former body, and with these he again laboureth for perfection, O joy of the Kurus.(43)

By that former practice he is irresistibly swept away. Only wishing to know yoga, even the seeker after yoga goeth beyond the Brâhmic world;[19] (44)

But the Yogî, labouring with assiduity, purified from sin, fully perfected through manifold births, he reacheth the supreme goal.(45)

The Yogî is greater than the ascetics; he is thought to be greater than even the wise; the Yogî is greater than the men of action; therefore become thou a Yogî, O Arjuna!(46)

And among all Yogîs, he who, full of faith, with the inner Self abiding in Me, adoreth Me, he is considered by Me to be the most completely harmonised.(47)

Thus in the glorious Upanishads of the Bhagavad-Gita, the science of the Eternal, the scripture of Yoga, in the dialogue between Shrî Krishna and Arjuna, the sixth discourse, entitled:

THE YOGA OF SELF-SUBDUAL.

---

[19] The Vedas.

SEVENTH DISCOURSE

The Nature of Divine Knowledge

Chapter 7 of the *Bhagavad Gita*, known as *Jnana Vijnana Yoga* (The Yoga of Knowledge and Wisdom), marks a shift in Krishna's teachings. While previous chapters focused on action and meditation, Krishna now introduces divine knowledge and wisdom as the means to truly understanding his nature and the ultimate reality. He explains that knowing him in both his material and transcendental aspects leads to liberation.

In this discourse, Krishna reveals his all-pervading presence and explains the **two types of knowledge**—*Jnana* (intellectual understanding) and *Vijnana* (realized wisdom). He also describes the **four types of seekers** who approach him and explains why devotion (*Bhakti Yoga*) is the highest path to attaining him.

The Twofold Nature of Krishna

Krishna begins by explaining that his divine energy pervades everything in the universe. He describes his **lower material nature (Prakriti)**, which consists of the eight elements—earth, water, fire, air, ether, mind, intellect, and ego. These elements form the basis of the physical world and bind living beings to illusion (*Maya*).

However, Krishna also possesses a higher, spiritual nature, which is beyond material existence. This **supreme energy (Para Prakriti)** is the eternal essence of all beings—the life force that sustains the universe. He explains that everything in existence, from the smallest creature to the highest gods, is **sustained by his divine presence**.

The Illusion of Maya and the Rare Seekers of Truth

Krishna explains that most people are trapped in **illusion (Maya),** unable to perceive the divine reality behind the material world. He describes how the **three Gunas (Sattva, Rajas, and Tamas)** influence human perception and keep beings bound to worldly desires. Only those who transcend this illusion can see Krishna as the ultimate reality behind all existence.

Among the countless beings in the world, Krishna states that only a rare few seek true spiritual knowledge, and even fewer attain complete realization. This reinforces the idea that spiritual awakening requires great effort, devotion, and divine grace.

The Four Types of Devotees

Krishna identifies **four kinds of seekers** who approach him:

1. **The distressed (Arta)** – Those who turn to God in times of suffering.

2. **The seekers of wealth (Artharthi)** – Those who pray for material gains.

3. **The inquisitive (Jijnasu)** – Those who seek spiritual knowledge out of curiosity.

4. **The wise (Jnani)** – Those who seek Krishna alone as the ultimate truth.

Among these, Krishna praises the **Jnani (the wise devotee)** as the highest, for they seek nothing but union with the divine. However, he reassures that all seekers, regardless of their motivations, are on the path toward him and will ultimately reach him through devotion and perseverance.

Why People Worship Other Gods

Krishna then explains why some people worship different deities instead of him. He clarifies that all forms of worship eventually lead to him, even when devotees seek other gods for temporary blessings. He describes how faith in different deities is granted by him, but those who worship temporary gods receive temporary results, while those who worship him attain eternal liberation.

This teaching emphasizes that Krishna is the ultimate source of all divine manifestations, making Bhakti (devotion to him) the most direct path to freedom from the cycle of birth and death.

Krishna as the Ultimate Reality

Krishna reveals that he is the source of all creation, the sustainer of the universe, and its final resting place. He describes himself as:

- The taste in water, the light of the sun and moon, and the **sacred syllable OM**.

- The strength of the strong, the wisdom of the wise, and the desire that is in harmony with dharma.

Through these descriptions, Krishna conveys that he is not limited to a specific form or place—he is present in all aspects of existence. Recognizing this truth leads to freedom from illusion and attachment to the material world.

The Power of Devotion and Knowledge

Chapter 7 marks a transition in Krishna's teachings. He shifts from emphasizing action and meditation to the supreme path of knowledge and devotion. By understanding Krishna's twofold nature, overcoming illusion, and surrendering to him with devotion, one moves beyond material existence and attains eternal liberation.

This chapter prepares Arjuna for the upcoming teachings, where Krishna will further explain the **supremacy of devotion (Bhakti Yoga)** and the direct path to realizing the divine. The key takeaway is that true wisdom lies in seeing Krishna as the essence of everything, and through unwavering devotion, one attains the ultimate goal of life—union with the divine.

The Blessed Lord said:

With the mind[1] clinging to me, O Pârtha, performing yoga, refuged in Me, how thou shalt without doubt know Me to the uttermost, that hear thou.(1)

I will declare to thee this knowledge and wisdom in its completeness, which, having known, there is nothing more here needeth to be known.(2)

Among thousands of men scarce one striveth for perfection; of the successful strivers scarce one knoweth Me in essence.(3)

---

[1] Manah.

Earth, water, fire, air, ether, Mind,[2] and Reason[3] also and Egoism[4]—these are the eightfold division of My nature.[5] (4)

This the inferior. Know My other nature,[5] the higher, the life-element, O mighty-armed, by which the universe is upheld.(5)

Know this to be the womb of all beings. I am the source of the forthgoing of the whole universe and likewise the place of its dissolving.(6)

There is naught whatsoever higher than I, O Dhananjaya. All this is threaded on Me, as rows of pearls on a string.(7)

I the sapidity in waters, O son of Kuntî, I the radiance in moon and sun; the Word of Power[6] in all the Vedas, sound in ether, and virility in men;(8)

The pure fragrance of earths and the brilliance in fire am I; the life in all beings am I, and the austerity in ascetics.(9)

Know Me, O Pârtha! as the eternal seed of all beings. I am the Reason[7] of the Reason[7]-endowed, the splendour of splendid things am I.(10)

And I the strength of the strong, devoid of desire and passion. In beings I am desire not contrary to duty,[8] O Lord of the Bharatas.(11)

The natures that are harmonious, active, slothful,[9] these know as from Me; not I in them, but they in me.(12)

All this world, deluded by these natures made by the three qualities,[10] knoweth not Me, above these, imperishable.(13)

---

[2] Manah.
[3] Buddhi.
[4] Ahañkâra.
[5] Prakriti, matter in the widest sense of the term, including all that has extension. The "Higher Prakriti," of the next verse, is sometimes called Daivîprakriti, the Light of the Logos.
[6] The Prañava, the Aum.
[7] Buddhi.
[8] Dharma.
[9] Sattvic, rajasic, tamasic, that is, those in whom one of the three qualities, Sattva, Rajah, Tamah, predominates.
[10] Gunas.

This divine illusion[11] of Mine, caused by the qualities,**Errore. Il segnalibro non è definito.** is hard to pierce; they who come to Me, they cross over this illusion.[11] (14)

The evil-doing, the deluded, the vilest men, they come not to Me, they whose wisdom is destroyed by illusion,[11] who have embraced the nature of demons.[12] (15)

Fourfold in division are the righteous ones who worship me, O Arjuna; the suffering, the seeker for knowledge, the self-interested and the wise, O Lord of the Bhâratas.(16)

Of these the wise, constantly harmonised, worshipping the One, is the best; I am supremely dear to the wise, and he is dear to Me.(17)

Noble are all these, but I hold the wise as verily Myself; he, Self united, is fixed on Me, the highest Path.(18)

At the close of many births the man full of wisdom cometh unto Me; "Vâsudeva[13] is all." saith he, the Mahâtmâ, very difficult to find.(19)

They whose wisdom hath been rent away by desires go forth to other Shining Ones, resorting to various external observances, according to their own natures.(20)

Any devotee who seeketh to worship with faith any such aspect, I verily bestow the unswerving faith of that man.(21)

He endowed with that faith, seeketh the worship of such a one, and from him he obtaineth his desires, I verily decreeing the benefits;(22)

Finite indeed the fruit that belongeth to those who are of small intelligence. To the Shining Ones go the worshippers of the Shining Ones, but my devotees come unto Me.(23)

Those devoid of Reason[14] think of Me, the unmanifest, as having manifestation, knowing not My supreme nature, imperishable, most excellent.(24)

---

[11] Mâyâ.
[12] Asuras, the opponents of the Suras or gods.
[13] A name of Shrî Krishna, as the son of Vasudeva.
[14] Buddhi.

Nor am I of all discovered, enveloped in My creation-illusion.[15] This deluded world knoweth Me not, the unborn, the imperishable.(25)

I know the beings that are past, that are present, that are to come, O Arjuna, but no one knoweth Me.(26)

By the delusion of the pairs of opposites, sprung from attraction and repulsion, O Bhârata, all beings walk this universe wholly deluded, O Parantapa.(27)

But those men of pure deeds, in whom sin is come to an end, they, freed from the delusive pairs of opposites, worship Me, steadfast in vows.(28)

They who, refuged in Me, strive for liberation from birth and death, they know the Eternal, the whole Self-knowledge, and all action.(29)

They who know Me as the knowledge of the elements, as that of the Shining Ones, and as that of the Sacrifice,[16] they harmonised in mind, know Me verily even in the time of forthgoing.[17] (30)

Thus in the glorious Upanishads of the Bhagavad-Gita, the science of the Eternal, the scripture of Yoga, the dialogue between Shrî Krishna and Arjuna, the seventh discourse, entitled:

THE YOGA OF DISCRIMINATIVE KNOWLEDGE.

---

[15] Yoga-Maya, the creative power of Yoga, all things being the thought-forms of the One.
[16] These six terms are: Brahman, Adhyâtma, Karma, Adhibhûta, Adhidaiva, Adhiyajña.
[17] Death—going forth from the body.

EIGHTH DISCOURSE

The Nature of Ultimate Reality

Chapter 8 of the *Bhagavad Gita*, known as *Akshara-Parabrahma Yoga* (The Yoga of the Imperishable Absolute), delves into the mysteries of life, death, and the eternal soul. Arjuna, now deeply engaged in Krishna's teachings, asks profound existential questions about the nature of Brahman (the Supreme Reality), the self (Atman), karma, and what happens after death.

In response, Krishna explains the path to liberation, the importance of remembering the divine at the moment of death, and the differences between temporary material existence and eternal spiritual existence. This chapter provides a roadmap for transcending mortality and attaining Krishna's divine abode.

Understanding Brahman, Atman, and Karma

Krishna first clarifies fundamental spiritual concepts:

- **Brahman** refers to the **Supreme, eternal reality** that pervades everything.

- **Adhyatma (the Self/Atman)** is the **individual soul**, which is an eternal fragment of the divine.

- **Karma** is **the force of actions** that binds living beings to the cycle of birth and death.

By understanding these principles, one can begin to detach from the fleeting nature of the material world and align with the **eternal truth**.

The Moment of Death and the Path to Liberation

Krishna emphasizes that the state of consciousness at the time of death determines the soul's next destination. Those who remember him in their final moments attain eternal union with him, escaping the cycle of rebirth. However, those attached to worldly desires return to the material realm, bound by their past karma.

He instructs Arjuna to cultivate constant remembrance of the divine through devotion and meditation, ensuring that at the moment of death, the mind remains fixed on Krishna. This teaching reinforces the practice of **Bhakti Yoga (devotional surrender)** as the most direct path to liberation.

The Two Paths After Death: Light and Darkness

Krishna describes **two distinct spiritual paths** that determine the fate of the soul after death:

1. **The Path of Light (Devayana)** – Those who attain self-realization and divine knowledge enter the eternal spiritual realm, beyond rebirth.

2. **The Path of Darkness (Pitriyana)** – Those still bound by desires and material attachments return to the cycle of reincarnation.

These paths symbolize spiritual evolution versus continued bondage. Krishna urges Arjuna to choose the path of wisdom and devotion to reach the highest state.

The Supreme Goal: Attaining Krishna's Eternal Abode

Krishna assures that those who devote themselves entirely to him transcend all worldly suffering. His divine abode is eternal, free from birth and death, beyond the limitations of time. Unlike the material universe, which undergoes constant creation and destruction, his realm is unchanging and everlasting.

He describes himself as the ultimate refuge, stating that all seekers—whether through knowledge, action, or devotion—will ultimately reach him. However, **devotion is the most direct and easiest path.**

The Imperishable Reality: Rising Above the Temporary World

Krishna contrasts the temporary nature of the material world with the eternity of the spiritual realm. He explains that the entire cosmos undergoes cycles of creation and dissolution, yet the soul remains untouched by these changes.

By understanding this, one can develop detachment from worldly illusions and cultivate devotion to the eternal divine. He urges Arjuna to recognize that the highest knowledge is not just intellectual understanding but deep, unwavering faith in the eternal nature of the soul and the supremacy of Krishna.

The Power of Devotion and Remembrance

Chapter 8 serves as a guide to spiritual transcendence, emphasizing that the key to liberation is unwavering devotion and remembrance of Krishna. By keeping one's mind fixed on the divine, both in life and at the moment of death, the soul is freed from rebirth and attains eternal peace.

This chapter deepens Krishna's previous teachings by revealing the ultimate goal of human existence: merging with the imperishable Brahman. As Arjuna absorbs these truths, Krishna prepares to elaborate further on Bhakti Yoga and the supreme path of loving devotion in the next discourse.

———————

Arjuna said:

What is that Eternal,[1] what Self-knowledge,[2] what Action,[3] O Purushottama? And what is declared to be the knowledge of the Elements,[4] what is called the knowledge of the Shining Ones?[5] (1)

What is the knowledge of Sacrifice[6] in this body, and how, O, Madhusûdana? And how, at the time of forthgoing art Thou known by the Self-controlled?(2)

The Blessed Lord said:

The indestructible, the supreme is the Eternal;[7] His essential nature is called Self-knowledge;[8] the emanation that causes the birth of beings is named Action;[9] (3)

---

[1] Brahman.
[2] Adhyâtma.
[3] Karma.
[4] Adhibhûta.
[5] Adhidaiva.
[6] Adhiyajña.
[7] Brahman.
[8] Adhyâtma.
[9] Karma.

Knowledge of the Elements[10] concerns My perishable nature, and knowledge of the Shining Ones[11] concerns the life-giving energy[12]; the knowledge of Sacrifice[13] tells of Me, as wearing the body, O best of living beings.(4)

And he who, casting off the body, goeth forth thinking upon Me only at the time of the end, he entereth into My being: there is no doubt of that.(5)

Whosoever at the end abandoneth the body, thinking upon any being, to that being only he goeth, O Kaunteya, ever to that conformed in nature.(6)

Therefore at all times think upon Me only and fight. With mind[14] and Reason[15] set on Me, without doubt thou shalt come to Me.(7)

With the mind[16] not wandering after aught else, harmonised by continual practice, constantly meditating, O Pârtha, one goeth to the Spirit supreme, divine.(8)

He who thinketh upon the Ancient, the Omniscient, the All-Ruler, minuter than the minute, the supporter of all, of form unimaginable, refulgent as the sun beyond the darkness,(9)

In the time of forthgoing, with unshaken mind,[17] fixed in devotion, by the power of yoga drawing together his life-breath in the centre of the two eyebrows, he goeth to this Spirit, supreme, divine.(10)

That which is declared indestructible by the Veda-knowers, that which the controlled and passion-free enter, that desiring which Brahmacharya[18] is performed, that path I will declare to thee with brevity.(11)

---

[10] Adhibhûta.
[11] Adhidaiva.
[12] Purusha, the male creative energy. The supreme Pursha is the Divine Man, the manifested God.
[13] Adhiyajña.
[14] Manah.
[15] Buddhi.
[16] Chetah.
[17] Manah.
[18] The vow of continence.

All the gates[19] closed, the mind confined in the heart, the life-breath fixed in his own head, concentrated by yoga,(12)

"Aum!" the one syllabled Eternal, reciting, thinking upon Me, he who goeth forth, abandoning the body, he goeth on the highest path.(13)

He who constantly thinketh upon Me, not thinking ever of another, of him I am easily reached, O Pârtha, of this ever-harmonised Yogî.(14)

Having come to Me, these Mahâtmâs come not again to birth, the place of pain, non-eternal; they have gone to the highest bliss.(15)

The worlds, beginning with the world of Brahmâ, they come and go, O Arjuna; but he who cometh unto Me, O Kaunteya, he knoweth birth no more.(16)

The people who know the day of Brahmâ, a thousand ages[20] in duration, and the night a thousand ages in ending, they know day and night.(17)

From the unmanifested all the manifested stream forth at the coming of day; at the coming of night they dissolve, even in That called the unmanifested.(18)

This multitude of beings, going forth repeatedly, is dissolved at the coming of night: by ordination, O Pârtha, it streams forth at the coming of day.(19)

Therefore verily there existeth, higher than that unmanifested, another unmanifested, eternal, which in the destroying of all beings, is not destroyed.(20

That unmanifested, "the Indestructible," It is called; It is named the highest Path. They who reach It return not. That is My supreme abode.(21)

He, the highest Spirit,[21] O Pârtha, may be reached by unswerving devotion to Him alone, in whom all beings abide, by whom all This[22] is pervaded.(22)

That time wherein going forth Yogîs return not, and also that wherein going forth they return, that time shall I declare to thee, O prince of the Bhâratas.(23)

_____

[19] The gates of the body, *i.e.*, the sense-organs.
[20] Yugas.
[21] Purusha.
[22] This, the universe, in opposition to that, the source of all.

Fire, light, day-time, the bright fortnight, the six months of the northern path[23]—then, going forth, the men who know the Eternal go to the Eternal.(24)

Smoke, night-time, the dark fortnight also, the six months of the southern path[23]—then the Yogî, obtaining the moonlight,[24] returneth.(25)

Light and darkness, these are thought to be the world's everlasting paths; by the one he goeth who returneth not, by the other he who returneth again.(26)

Knowing these paths, O Pârtha, the Yogi is nowise perplexed. Therefore in all times be firm in yoga, O Arjuna.(27)

The fruit of meritorious deeds, attached in the Vedas to sacrifices, to austerities, and also to almsgiving, the Yogî passeth all these by having known this, and goeth to the supreme and ancient Seat.(28)

Thus in the glorious Upanishads of the Bhagavad-Gita, the science of the Eternal, the scripture of Yoga, the dialogue between Shrî Krishna and Arjuna, the eighth discourse, entitled:

THE YOGA OF THE INDESCTRUCTIBLE SUPREME ETERNAL.

---

[23] Of the sun.
[24] The Lunar, or astral body. Until this is slain the soul returns to birth.

NINTH DISCOURSE

The Most Confidential Knowledge

Chapter 9 of the *Bhagavad Gita*, known as *Raja-Vidya Raja-Guhya Yoga* (The Yoga of Royal Knowledge and Royal Mystery), is one of the most profound chapters in the entire text. Krishna declares that he will now reveal the highest and most secret knowledge—a wisdom that leads directly to liberation. This knowledge is called "royal" because it is the king of all wisdom, and a mystery because it is known only to those who approach it with faith and devotion.

In this chapter, Krishna shifts his emphasis toward **Bhakti Yoga**, the path of devotion, explaining why those who surrender to him with love attain the highest realization. He also reveals his divine immanence, explaining how he pervades all things while remaining beyond them.

Faith and Devotion as the Key to Liberation

Krishna begins by stating that those who have faith and are devoted to him attain true wisdom and liberation. He explains that many people fail to recognize his divine nature due to ignorance and doubt, causing them to remain bound to the cycle of birth and death. Only those who approach him with an open heart and sincere devotion can grasp the true nature of reality.

Unlike the previous chapters, which emphasized action and knowledge, Krishna now presents devotion as the supreme path. He reassures Arjuna that even the simplest acts of love and worship—if offered with sincerity—lead to ultimate liberation.

Krishna's All-Pervading Presence

Krishna describes his omnipresence, explaining that he is both immanent and transcendent. He pervades the universe, yet remains beyond it. He is the sustaining force behind all creation, yet he is not limited by it.

He uses the analogy of air resting in space to illustrate this paradox—everything exists within him, yet he is not bound by anything. This reinforces the idea that God is both personal and impersonal, accessible to those who seek him with devotion but beyond comprehension for those who rely solely on intellectual reasoning.

The Fate of Worshippers of Other Gods

Krishna acknowledges that people worship different deities, each seeking various material benefits. However, he explains that all forms of worship ultimately lead to him because he is the source of all divine manifestations. Those who worship lesser gods receive temporary results, while those who devote themselves solely to Krishna attain eternal fulfillment.

This teaching clarifies that while other paths may yield benefits, only pure devotion to the Supreme Divine leads to complete liberation from the cycle of birth and death.

Simple Devotion is Supreme

One of the most famous verses in this chapter is Krishna's assurance that he accepts even the simplest offerings if given with love:

"Whoever offers me a leaf, a flower, a fruit, or water with love and devotion, I accept it."

This verse highlights the **accessibility of Bhakti Yoga**—one does not need wealth, rituals, or scholarly knowledge to reach God. What matters is the sincerity and purity of the heart.

Krishna also promises that anyone, regardless of background, caste, or social status, can attain liberation through devotion. This marks a revolutionary teaching, rejecting rigid societal divisions and emphasizing the universal accessibility of divine grace.

The Supreme Promise: Absolute Protection

In one of the most comforting teachings of the *Bhagavad Gita*, Krishna proclaims:

"Abandon all forms of dharma and surrender completely to me. I will deliver you from all sins. Do not fear."

This declaration emphasizes **absolute surrender** (*Sharanagati*) as the highest spiritual act. Krishna reassures Arjuna that those who seek refuge in him need not worry about karma, sins, or past mistakes—he will personally ensure their liberation.

The Power of Bhakti Yoga

Chapter 9 establishes devotion as the most direct and powerful path to liberation. Unlike the complex practices of knowledge or austerities, Bhakti Yoga is accessible to all—rich or poor, learned or uneducated.

Krishna's message is clear: love and surrender to him bring the highest realization. As the discourse continues, Krishna will further elaborate on his divine nature, leading Arjuna toward an even deeper understanding of the ultimate truth in the following chapters.

The Blessed Lord said:

To thee, the uncarping, verily shall I declare this profoundest Secret, wisdom with knowledge combined, which, having known, thou shalt be freed from evil.(1)

Kingly Science, kingly Secret, supreme Purifier, this; intuitional, according to righteousness,[1] very easy to perform, imperishable.(2)

Men without faith in this knowledge,[1] O Parantapa, not reaching Me, return to the paths of this world of death.(3)

By Me all this world is pervaded in My unmanifested aspect; all beings have root in Me, I am not rooted in them.(4)

Nor have beings root in Me; behold My sovereign Yoga! The support of beings, yet not rooted in beings, My Self their efficient cause.(5)

As the mighty air everywhere moving is rooted in the Ether,[2] so all beings rest rooted in Me—thus know thou.(6)

All beings, O Kaunteya, enter my lower nature[3] at the end of a world-age;[4] at the beginning of a world-age[4] again I emanate them.(7)

Hidden in Nature,[3] which is mine own, I emanate again and again all this multitude of beings, helpless, by the force of Nature[3].(8)

---

[1] Dharma.
[2] Akâsha.
[3] Prakriti.
[4] Kalpa, a period of activity, of manifestation.

Nor do these works bind me, O Dhananjaya, enthroned on high unattached to actions.(9)

Under Me as supervisor, Nature[3] sends forth the moving and unmoving: because of this, O Kaunteya, the universe revolves.(10)

The foolish disregard Me, when clad in human semblance, ignorant of My supreme nature, the great Lord of beings;(11)

Empty of hope, empty of deeds, empty of wisdom, senseless, partaking of the deceitful, brutal and demoniacal nature.[5] (12)

Verily the Mahâtmâs, O Partha, partaking of My divine nature,[5] worship with unwavering mind,[6] having known Me, the imperishable source of beings.(13)

Always magnifying Me, strenuous, firm in vows, prostrating themselves before Me, they worship Me with devotion ever harmonised.(14

Others also, sacrificing with the sacrifice of wisdom, worship Me as the One and the Manifold everywhere present.(15)

I the ablation; I the sacrifice; I the ancestral offering; I the fire-giving herb; the mantram I; I also the butter; I the fire; the burnt-offering I;(16)

I the Father of this universe, the Mother, the Supporter, the Grandsire, the Holy one to be known, the Word of Power,[7] and also the Rik, Sâma, and Yajur,[8] (17)

The Path, Husband, Lord, Witness, Abode, Shelter, Lover, Origin, Dissolution, Foundation, house, Seed imperishable.(18)

I give heat; I hold back and send forth the rain; immortality and also death, being and non-being[9] am I, Arjuna.(19)

---

[5] Prakriti. The Tamasic Guna, or the dark quality of Prakriti, characterises the beings here spoken of as rakshasic and asuric. Rakshasas were semi-human beings, brutal and bloodthirsty; Asuras were the opponents of the Devas.

[6] Manah.

[7] Aumkara, the Sacred Word, Aum.

[8] The Three Vedas.

[9] Sat and Asat, the final pair of opposites, beyond which is only the One.

The knowers of the three,[10] the Soma-drinkers, the purified from sin, worshipping Me with sacrifice, pray of Me the way to heaven; they, ascending to the holy world of the Ruler of the Shining Ones, eat in heaven the divine feasts of the Shining Ones.(20)

They, having enjoyed the spacious heaven-world, their holiness withered,[11] come back to this world of death. Following the virtues enjoined by the three,[12] desiring desires, they obtain the transitory.(21)

To those men who worship Me alone thinking of no other, to those ever harmonious, I bring full security.(22)

Even the devotees of other Shining Ones, who worship full of faith, they also worship Me, O son of Kuntî, though contrary to the ancient rule.(23)

I am indeed the enjoyer of all sacrifices and also the Lord, but they know Me not in Essence, and hence they fall.(24)

They who worship the Shining Ones go to the Shining Ones; to the Ancestors[13] go the Ancestor-worshippers; to the Elements[14] go those who sacrifice to Elementals; but My worshippers come unto Me.(25)

He who offereth to Me with devotion a leaf, a flower, a fruit, water, that I accept from the striving self, offered as it is with devotion.(26)

Whatsoever thou doest, whatsoever thou eatest, whatsoever thou offerest, whatsoever thou givest, whatsoever thou doest of austerity, O Kaunteya, do thou that as an offering unto Me.(27)

Thus shalt thou be liberated from the bonds of action, yielding good and evil fruits; thyself harmonised by the yoga of renunciation, thou shalt come unto Me when set free.(28)

The same am I to all beings; there is none hateful to Me nor dear. They verily who worship Me with devotion, they are in Me, and I also in them.(29)

---

[10] The Three Vedas.
[11] The fruit of their good deeds finished, their reward exhausted.
[12] Vedas.
[13] Pitris.
[14] Bhutas, Elementals or nature-spirits.

Even if the most sinful worship Me, with undivided heart, he too must be accounted righteous, for he hath rightly resolved;(30)

Speedily he becometh dutiful and goeth to eternal peace; O Kaunteya, know thou for certain that My devotee perisheth never.(31)

They who take refuge with Me, O Partha, though of the womb of sin, women, Vaishyas,[15] even Shûdras,[16] they also tread the highest path.(32)

How much rather then holy Brâhmanas and devoted royal saints; having obtained this transient joyless world, worship thou Me.(33)

On Me fix thy mind,[17] be devoted to Me; sacrifice to Me; prostrate thyself before Me; harmonised thus in the Self, thou shalt come unto Me, having Me as thy supreme goal.(34)

Thus in the glorious Upanishads of the Bhagavad-Gita, the science of the Eternal, the scripture of Yoga, the dialogue between Shrî Krishna and Arjuna, the ninth discourse, entitled:

THE YOGA OF THE KINGLY SCIENCE AND THE KINGLY SECRET.

---

[15] The third, the merchant caste.
[16] The fourth, the manual labouring class.
[17] Manah.

TENTH DISCOURSE

Krishna as the Source of All

Chapter 10 of the *Bhagavad Gita*, known as *Vibhuti Yoga* (The Yoga of Divine Glories), presents Krishna revealing his infinite manifestations and divine opulence. Here, Krishna explains that everything extraordinary in the universe is but a reflection of his divine power. This chapter deepens Arjuna's understanding of Krishna's supreme position, showing that all that is great, beautiful, and powerful originates from him.

Arjuna, having absorbed Krishna's teachings on devotion and surrender, now seeks to understand Krishna's divine manifestations. Krishna responds by listing his glories (*Vibhutis*), demonstrating that he is the essence of all things majestic and magnificent.

The Supreme Truth and Divine Manifestations

Krishna begins by reiterating that he is the ultimate cause of all creation. He declares that all beings and elements originate from him, yet he remains beyond them. He is both the unmanifest source and the immanent presence within all things. This teaching reinforces that **Krishna is not merely a god among gods, but the Supreme Divine Reality**.

He emphasizes that those who realize his divine nature attain unwavering devotion (Bhakti Yoga), their minds absorbed in him with love and reverence. He assures that to those who worship him with sincerity, he grants divine wisdom (Jnana) and removes the darkness of ignorance.

The Limitless Expressions of Krishna's Power

Krishna lists numerous **Vibhutis (divine manifestations)** to illustrate his omnipresence. He declares that among celestial bodies, he is the sun; among mountains, he is the Himalayas; among rivers, he is the Ganges. These examples show that wherever there is greatness, splendor, or supremacy, it is a direct reflection of Krishna's divine power.

Some of the key manifestations Krishna names include:

- **Among the Vedas, he is the Sama Veda** (representing the essence of knowledge and melody).

- **Among warriors, he is Rama** (the ideal embodiment of righteousness and strength).

- **Among sages, he is Vyasa** (the great compiler of the scriptures).

- **Among sacrifices, he is Japa (silent meditation)** (showing that inner devotion is the highest offering).

Through these examples, Krishna demonstrates that his presence is everywhere, from nature to human virtues and divine figures. His immanence in the world makes it possible to recognize and worship him through admiration and reverence for creation itself.

Arjuna's Response: Total Devotion

Upon hearing Krishna's revelations, Arjuna is overwhelmed with awe and gratitude. He now fully acknowledges Krishna as the Supreme Being, beyond comprehension and beyond all other deities. His devotion deepens as he realizes that **Krishna alone is the ultimate reality, the source of all power and wisdom.**

Arjuna humbly asks Krishna to elaborate further on how he should meditate on his divine presence. Krishna, ever compassionate, continues to describe his infinite manifestations, reminding Arjuna that it is through devotion and love that one can truly perceive the divine.

Krishna's Final Declaration: The Pinnacle of His Glory

As the discourse reaches its climax, Krishna makes a bold proclamation:

"But what need is there, Arjuna, for all this detailed knowledge? With a single fragment of myself, I pervade and sustain this entire universe."

With this statement, Krishna conveys that his divine power is boundless, and that the entire universe exists merely through a fraction of his being. This revelation instills both humility and devotion in Arjuna, reinforcing that the supreme goal of life is to surrender completely to Krishna's divine will.

Recognizing Divinity in All Things

Krishna's message is clear: spiritual realization is not just about knowledge, but about seeing the divine in all aspects of life. For Arjuna, this chapter strengthens his conviction that **Krishna is the Supreme Truth**, preparing him for the next revelation—the grand **Vishvarupa Darshana (the Universal Form)** in the following discourse.

———

The Blessed Lord said:

Again, O mighty-armed, hear thou My supreme word, that, desiring thy welfare, I will declare to thee who art beloved.(1)

The multitude of the Shining Ones, or the great Rishis,[1] know not my forthcoming, for I am the beginning of all the Shining Ones and the great Rishis.(2)

He who knoweth Me, unborn, beginningless, the great Lord of the world, he among mortals without delusion, is liberated from all sin.(3)

Reason,[2] wisdom, non-illusion, forgiveness, truth, self-restraint, calmness, pleasure, pain, existence, non-existence, fear, and also courage(4)

Harmlessness, equanimity, content, austerity, almsgiving, fame and obloquy are the various characteristics of beings issuing from Me.(5)

The seven great Rishis, the ancient Four,[3] and also the Manus,[4] were born of My nature, and mind; of them this race was generated.(6)

He who knows in essence that sovereignty and yoga of Mine, he is harmonised by unfaltering yoga; there is no doubt thereof.(7)

I am the Generator of all; all evolves from Me; understanding thus, the wise adore Me in rapt emotion.(8)

Mindful of Me, their life hidden in Me, illumining each other, ever conversing about Me, they are content and joyful.(9)

To these, ever harmonious, worshipping in love, I give the yoga of discrimination[5] by which they come unto Me.(10)

---

[1] A Rishi is a man who has completed his human evolution, but who remains in the super-physical regions in touch with the earth, in order to help humanity.
[2] Buddhi.
[3] The four Kumaras, or Virgin Youths, the highest in the occult Hierarchy of this earth.
[4] The heads and legislators of a race.
[5] Buddhi-Yoga.

Out of pure compassion for them, dwelling within their Self, I destroy the ignorance-born darkness by the shining lamp of wisdom.(11)

Arjuna said:

Thou art the supreme Eternal, the supreme Abode, the supreme Purity, eternal divine man, primeval Deity, unborn, the Lord!(12)

All the Rishis have thus acclaimed Thee, as also the divine Rishi, Nârada; so Asita, Devala, and Vyâsa; and now Thou Thyself tellest it me.(13)

All this I believe true that Thou sayest to me, O Keshava. Thy manifestation, O Blessed Lord, neither Shining Ones nor Dânavas[6] comprehend.(14)

Thyself indeed knowest Thyself by Thyself, O Purushottama; Source of beings, Lord of beings, Shining One of Shining Ones, Ruler of the world!(15)

Deign to tell without reserve of Thine own divine glories, by which glories Thou remainest, pervading these worlds.(16)

How may I know thee, O Yogi, by constant meditation? In what, in what aspects art Thou to be thought of by me, O blessed Lord?(17)

In detail tell me again of Thy yoga and glory, O Janardana; for me there is never satiety in hearing thy life-giving words.(18)

The Blessed Lord said:

Blessed be thou! I will declare to thee My divine glory by its chief characteristics, O best of the Kurus; there is no end to details of Me.(19)

I, O Gudakesha, am the Self, seated in the heart of all beings; I am the beginning, the middle, and also the end of all beings.(20)

Of the Adityas I am Vishnu; of radiances the glorious sun; I am Marîchi of the Maruts; of the asterisms the Moon am I.(21)

Of the Vedas I am the Sâma-Veda; I am Vâsava of the Shining Ones; and of the senses I am the mind[7]; I am of living beings the intelligence[8].(22)

---

[6] Demigods, in the Greek sense.
[7] Manah.
[8] Chetana.

And of the Rudras[9] Shañkara am I; Vittesha of the Yakshas and Râkshasas[10]; and of the Vasus[9] I am Pâvaka; Meru of high mountains am I.(23)

And know Me, O Pârtha, of household priests the chief, Brihaspati: of generals I am Skanda; of lakes I am the ocean.(24)

Of the great Rishis Bhṛigu; of speech I am the one syllable[11]; of sacrifices I am the sacrifice of silent repetitions[12]; of immovable things the Himâlaya.(25)

Asvattha of all tree; and of divine Rishis Nârada; of Gandharvas[13] Chitraratha; of the perfected the Muni Kapila.(26)

Uchchaishravas of horses know me, nectar-born[14]; Airâvata of lordly elephants, and of men the Monarch.(27)

Of weapons I am the thunderbolt; of cows I am Kâmadhuk; I am Kandarpa of the progenitors; of serpents Vâsuki am I.(28)

And I am Ananta of Nâgas[15], Varuna of sea-dwellers I; and of ancestors Aryaman; Yama of governors am I.(29)

And I am Prahlâda of Daityas;[16] of calculators Time am I; and of wild beasts I the imperial beast;[17] and Vainateya of birds.(30)

Of purifiers I am the wind; Rama of warriors I; and I am Makara of fishes; of streams the Gangâ am I.

Of creations the beginning and the ending, and also the middle am I, O Arjuna. Of sciences the science concerning the Self; the speech of orators I.(32)

---

[9] Celestial beings.
[10] Semi-human beings.
[11] Om.
[12] Japa.
[13] Celestial Singers.
[14] Amrita, the nectar of immortality.
[15] Serpents, who were Teachers of Wisdom.
[16] Semi-human beings.
[17] Lion.

Of letters the letter A I am, and the duality of a compound[18]; I also everlasting Time; I the Supporter, whose face turns everywhere.(33)

And all-devouring Death am I, and the origin of all to come; and of feminine qualities, fame, prosperity, speech, memory, intelligence, constancy, forgiveness.(34)

Of hymns also Brihatsâman; Gâyatrî of metres am I; of months I am Mârgasîrsha; of seasons the flowery.(35)

I am the gambling of the cheat, and the splendour of splendid things I; I am victory, I am determination, and the truth of the truthful I.(36)

Of the Vṛishnis[19] Vâsudeva am I; of the Pândavas[19] Dhananjaya; of the Sages[20] also I am Vyâsa; of poets Ushanâ the Bard.(37)

Of rulers I am the sceptre; of those that seek victory I am statesmanship; and of secrets I am also silence; the knowledge of knowers am I.(38)

And whatsoever is the seed of all beings, that am I, O Arjuna; nor is there aught, moving or unmoving, that may exist bereft of Me.(39)

There is no end of My divine powers, O Parantapa. What has been declared is illustrative of My infinite glory.(40)

Whatsoever is glorious, good, beautiful, and mighty, understand thou that to go forth from a fragment of My splendour.(41)

But what is the knowledge of all these details to thee, O Arjuna? Having pervaded this whole universe with one fragment of Myself, I remain.(42)

Thus in the glorious Upanishads of the Bhagavad-Gita, the science of the Eternal, the scripture of Yoga, the dialogue between Shri Krishna and Arjuna, the tenth discourse, entitled:

THE YOGA OF SOVEREIGNTY.

---

[18] Dvanda.
[19] A family, or clan, among the Hindus.
[20] Munis.

ELEVENTH DISCOURSE

Arjuna's Desire to See Krishna's True Form

Chapter 11 of the *Bhagavad Gita*, known as *Vishvarupa Darshana Yoga* (The Yoga of the Universal Form), marks a dramatic turning point in Krishna's teachings. Until now, Krishna has described his divine nature through words, but Arjuna, filled with devotion and curiosity, wishes to see Krishna's supreme, cosmic form. In response, Krishna grants him divine vision, revealing a form beyond human comprehension—a vast, all-encompassing manifestation that displays the infinite nature of the Divine.

This chapter conveys the magnitude of Krishna's power, reinforcing that he is not merely a god among many, but the Supreme Reality itself. The experience profoundly impacts Arjuna, filling him with awe, reverence, and even fear.

Krishna's Revelation: The Universal Form

Krishna grants Arjuna divine sight so he can perceive his true nature. What Arjuna sees is indescribable—a vision of infinite faces, countless arms, celestial ornaments, and radiant splendor, stretching in all directions. Within this form, Arjuna beholds the entire universe—the past, present, and future—unfolding simultaneously. He sees divine beings, the forces of nature, and countless souls moving toward their destiny. The sheer vastness of Krishna's form transcends all human understanding.

Krishna's **Universal Form (Vishvarupa)** embodies both creation and destruction, showing Arjuna the unstoppable cycle of life, death, and rebirth. This revelation confirms that Krishna is the ultimate reality, the source and end of all existence.

The Terrifying Aspect of the Universal Form

As Arjuna continues to witness Krishna's form, his awe turns into deep fear. He sees powerful warriors—both friend and foe—being consumed by Krishna's all-devouring mouths, symbolizing the inevitable destruction of all beings through time. This vision is not just a display of divine grandeur; it also reveals Krishna as **Kala (Time), the great force that governs all destinies**.

79

Krishna declares:

"I am Time, the great destroyer of the world. I have come here to engage all beings. Even without your participation, all these warriors will perish."

With these words, Krishna assures Arjuna that the outcome of the war is already determined—his role is simply to act as an instrument of divine will. This teaching emphasizes detachment from results, reinforcing the lesson of Karma Yoga (selfless action).

Arjuna's Overwhelming Devotion and Surrender

Overcome with awe, humility, and fear, Arjuna bows before Krishna, recognizing him as the Supreme Being beyond all gods, beyond all conceptions of divinity. He realizes that Krishna is the origin of all creation and the force driving the universe.

Arjuna then apologizes for any past familiarity or mistakes in his relationship with Krishna, now understanding his true, divine identity. He humbly requests Krishna to return to his more familiar human form, as the Universal Form is too overwhelming to bear.

Krishna's Return to His Compassionate Form

Seeing Arjuna's fear and reverence, Krishna reassures him and resumes his four-armed and then two-armed form, restoring Arjuna's sense of calm. He explains that this vision is rarely granted, attainable only through unwavering devotion (Bhakti Yoga).

Krishna declares:

"Only by undivided devotion can I be truly known, seen, and entered into."

Here, Krishna establishes Bhakti Yoga as the highest path, emphasizing that devotion, rather than knowledge or austerities, is the key to realizing the Divine.

The Ultimate Lesson of the Universal Form

Chapter 11 presents Krishna's most awe-inspiring revelation, forcing Arjuna—and the reader—to confront the vastness, power, and inevitability of divine will. The vision teaches:

- **Krishna is beyond form yet present in all forms**—both terrifying and compassionate.

- **Time (Kala) is unstoppable**—all things arise and dissolve within the Divine.

- **Surrender and devotion**—only through Bhakti can one truly experience Krishna's essence.

This chapter marks a pivotal moment in Arjuna's spiritual journey. Having witnessed the Universal Form, he is now prepared to embrace his duty without doubt, strengthened by Krishna's supreme revelation. The next discourse will continue exploring the path of devotion as the ultimate means to liberation.

Arjuna said:

This word of the supreme Secret concerning the Self, Thou hast spoken out of compassion; by this my delusion is taken away.(1)

The production and destruction of beings have been heard by me in detail from Thee, O Lotus-eyed, and also Thy imperishable greatness.(2)

O supreme Lord,[1] even as Thou describest Thyself, O best of beings, I desire to see Thy Form omnipotent.(3)

If Thou thinkest that by me It can be seen, O Lord, Lord of Yoga, then show me Thine imperishable Self.(4)

The Blessed Lord said:

Behold, O Pârtha, a Form of Me, a hundredfold, a thousandfold, various in kind, divine, various in colours and shapes.(5)

Behold the Âdityas, the Vasus, the Rudras, the two Ashvins and also the Maruts[2]; behold many marvels never seen ere this, O Bhârata.(6)

Here, to-day, behold the whole universe, movable and immovable, standing in one in My body, O Gudâkesha, with aught else thou desirest to see.(7)

But verily thou art not able to behold Me with these thine eyes; the divine eye I give unto thee. Behold My sovereign Yoga.

---

[1] Ishvara, the Creator and Ruler of a Universe.
[2] Various classes of Celestial Beings.

Sanjaya said:

Having thus spoken, O King, the great Lord of Yoga, Hari, showed to Pârtha His supreme Form as Lord.[3] (9)

With many mouths and eyes, with many visions of marvel, with many divine ornaments, with many upraised divine weapons;(10)

Wearing divine necklaces and vestures, anointed with divine unguents, the God all-marvellous, boundless, with face turned everywhere.(11)

If the splendour of a thousand suns were to blaze out together in the sky, that might resemble the glory of that Mahâtman.(12)

There Pândava beheld the whole universe, divided into manifold parts, standing in one in the body of the Deity of Deities.(13)

Then he, Dhananjaya, overwhelmed with astonishment, his hair upstanding, bowed down his head to the Shining One, and with joined palms spake.(14)

Arjuna said:

Within Thy Form, O God, the Gods I see,
All grades of beings with distinctive marks;
Brahma, the Lord, upon His lotus-throne,
The Rishis all, and Serpents, the Divine.(15)

With mouths, eyes, arms, breasts multitudinous,
I see Thee everywhere, unbounded Form.
Beginning, middle, end, nor source of Thee,
Infinite Lord, infinite Form, I find;(16)

Shining, a mass of splendour everywhere,
With discus, mace, tiara, I behold:
Blazing as fire, as sun dazzling the gaze,
From all sides in the sky, immeasurable.(17)

Lofty beyond all thought, unperishing,
Thou treasure-house supreme, all-immanent;
Eternal Dharma's changeless Guardian, Thou;
As immemorial Man I think of Thee.(18)

---

[3] Ishvara.

Nor source, nor midst, nor end; infinite force,
Unnumbered arms, the sun and moon Thine eyes

I see Thy face, as sacrificial fire
Blazing, its splendour burneth up the worlds.(19)

By Thee alone are filled the earth, the heavens,
And all the regions that are stretched between;
The triple worlds sink down, O mighty One,
Before Thine awful manifested Form.(20)

To Thee the troops of Suras enter in,
Some with joined palms in awe invoking Thee;
Banded Maharshis, Siddhas, cry: "All hail"!
Chanting Thy praises with resounding songs.(21)

Rudras, Vasus, Sâdhyas and Adityas,
Vishvas, the Ashvins, Maruts, Ushmapas,
Gandharvas, Yakshas, Siddhas, Asuras,[4]
In wondering multitudes beholding Thee.(22)

Thy mighty Form, with many mouths and eyes,
Long armed, with thighs and feet innumerate,
Vast-bosomed, set with many fearful teeth,
The worlds see terror-struck, as also I.(23)

Radiant, Thou touchest heaven, rainbow-hued,
With opened mouths and shining vast-orbed eyes.
My inmost self is quaking, having seen,
My strength is withered, Vishnu, and my peace.(24)

Like Time's destroying flames I see Thy teeth,
Upstanding, spread within expanded jaws;
Nought know I anywhere, no shelter find;
Mercy, O God! re of all the worlds!(25)

The sons of Dhṛitarâshtra, and with them
The multitude of all these kings of earth,
Bhîshma, and Drona, Sûta's royal son,
And all the noblest warriors of our hosts,(26)

---

[4] Names of various grades of super-physical beings.

Into Thy gaping mouths they hurrying rush,
Tremendous-toothed and terrible to see;
Some caught within the gaps between Thy teeth
Are seen, their heads to powder crushed and ground.(27)

As river-floods impetuously rush,
Hurling their waters into ocean's lap,
So fling themselves into Thy flaming mouths,
In haste, these mighty men, these lords of earth.(28)

As moths with quickened speed will headlong fly
Into a flaming light, to fall destroyed,
So also these, in haste precipitate,
Enter within Thy mouths destroyed to fall.(29)

On every side, all-swallowing, fiery-tongued,
Thou lickest up mankind, devouring all;
The glory filleth space: the universe
Is burning, Vishnu, with Thy blazing rays.(30)

Reveal Thy Self; what awful Form art Thou?
I worship Thee! Have mercy, God supreme!
Thine inner Being I am fain to know;
This Thy forth-streaming Life bewilders me.(31)

Time am I, laying desolate the world,
Made manifest on earth to slay mankind!
Not one of all these warriors ranged for strife
Escapeth death; thou shalt alone survive.(32)

Therefore stand up! win for thyself renown,
Conquer thy foes, enjoy the wealth filled realm,
By Me they are already overcome,
Be thou the outward cause, left-handed one.(33)

Drona and Bhîshma and Jayadratha,
Karna, and all the other warriors here,
Are slain by Me. Destroy them fearlessly.
Fight! thou shalt crush thy rivals in the field.(34)

Sanjaya said:

Having heard these words of Keshava, he who weareth a diadem, with joined palms, quaking and prostrating himself, spake again to Krishna, stammering with fear, casting down his face.(35)

Arjuna said:

Hrishîkesha! in Thy magnificence
Rightly the world rejoiceth, hymning Thee;
The Râkshasas to every quarter fly
In fear; the hosts of Siddhas prostrate fall.(36)

How should they otherwise, O loftiest Self!
First Cause! Brahmâ Himself less great than Thou.
Infinite, God of Gods, home of all worlds,
Unperishing, Sat, Asat,[5] That supreme!(37)

First of the Gods, most ancient Man Thou art.
Supreme receptacle of all that lives;
Knower and known, the dwelling-place on high;
In Thy vast Form the universe is spread.(38)

Thou art Vâyu and Yama, Agni, moon,
Varuna, Father, Grandsire of all;
Hail, hail to Thee! a thousand times all hail!
Hail unto Thee! again, again all hail!(39)

Prostrate in front of Thee, prostrate behind;
Prostrate on every side to Thee, O All.
In power boundless, measureless in strength,
Thou holdest all: then Thou Thyself art All.(40)

If, thinking Thee but friend, importunate,
O Krishna! or O Yâdava! O friend!
I cried, unknowing of Thy majesty,
And careless in the fondness of my love;(41)

If jesting I irreverence showed to Thee,
At play, reposing, sitting or at meals,
Alone, O sinless One, or with my friends,
Forgive my error, O Thou boundless One.(42)

---

[5] Being, Non-Being.

Father of worlds, of all that moves and stands,
Worthier of reverence than the Guru's self,

There is none like to Thee. Who passeth Thee?
Pre-eminent Thy power in all the worlds.(43)

Therefore I fall before Thee; with my body
I worship as it fitting; bless Thou me.
As father with the son, as friend with friend,
With the beloved as lover, bear with me.(44)

I have seen that which none hath seen before,
My heart is glad, yet faileth me for fear;
Show me, O God, Thine other Form again—
Mercy, O God of Gods, home of all worlds—(45)

Diademed, mace and discus in Thy hand.
Again I fain would see Thee as before;
Put on again Thy four-armed shape, O Lord,
O thousand-armed, of forms innumerate.(46)

The Blessed Lord said:

Arjuna, by My favour thou hast seen,
This loftiest Form by yoga's self revealed!

Radiant, all-penetrating, endless, first,
That none except thyself hath ever seen.(47)

Nor sacrifice, nor Vedas, alms, nor works,
Nor sharp austerity, nor study deep,
Can win the vision of this Form for man,
Foremost of Kurus, thou alone hast seen.(48)

Be not bewildered, be thou not afraid,
Because thou hast beheld this awful Form;
Cast fear away, and let thy heart rejoice;
Behold again Mine own familiar shape.(49)

Sanjaya said:

Vâsudeva, having thus spoken to Arjuna, again manifested His own Form, and consoled the terrified one, the Mahâtman again assuming a gentle form.(50)

Arjuna said:

Beholding again Thy gentle human Form, O Janârdana, I am now collected, and am restored to my own nature.(51)

The Blessed Lord said:

This Form of Mine beholden by thee is very hard to see. Verily the Shining Ones ever long to behold this form.(52)

Nor can I be seen as thou hast seen Me by the Vedas, nor by austerities, nor by alms, or by offerings;(53)

But by devotion to Me alone I may thus be perceived, Arjuna, and known and seen in essence, and entered, O Parantapa.(54)

He who doeth actions for Me, whose supreme good I am, My devotee, freed from attachment without hatred of any being, he cometh unto Me, O Pândava.(55)

Thus in the glorious Upanishads of the Bhagavad-Gita, the science of the Eternal, the scripture of Yoga, the dialogue between Shri Krishna and Arjuna, the eleventh discourse, entitled:

THE YOGA OF THE VISION OF THE UNIVERSAL FORM.

TWELFTH DISCOURSE

The Supremacy of Bhakti Yoga

Chapter 12 of the *Bhagavad Gita*, known as *Bhakti Yoga* (The Yoga of Devotion), is a pivotal discourse in which Krishna declares **devotion (bhakti) as the highest and most accessible path to spiritual liberation**. After witnessing Krishna's Universal Form, Arjuna is deeply moved and seeks clarity on the nature of the ideal devotee and the best way to attain the divine.

Arjuna asks Krishna whether worshiping a formless, impersonal Brahman or worshiping Krishna as the personal God is superior. Krishna responds by affirming that both paths lead to liberation, but devotion to the personal divine is easier and more fulfilling for most seekers. This chapter provides a simple yet profound guide to Bhakti Yoga, emphasizing that love, surrender, and faith are the key elements of the spiritual journey.

Personal Worship vs. Impersonal Worship

Krishna explains that those who worship him with unwavering faith and devotion are most dear to him. While the path of Jnana Yoga (knowledge of the formless Brahman) is valid, it is difficult, requiring immense discipline, detachment, and intellectual effort. Worshiping the unmanifest, Krishna says, is challenging because it requires the seeker to transcend all sensory perception and material attachment.

On the other hand, Bhakti Yoga is direct and accessible to all. By worshiping Krishna with love and devotion, a seeker can cultivate a personal relationship with the divine, making spiritual progress effortless and joyful. Krishna reassures that he personally takes care of his devotees, ensuring their ultimate liberation.

The Qualities of an Ideal Devotee

Krishna then describes the attributes of a true devotee, outlining the virtues that make one beloved to him. A devotee is free from ego, hatred, and selfish desires, remaining calm, patient, and compassionate. Krishna highlights qualities such as:

- Equanimity in joy and sorrow

- Absence of pride and possessiveness

- Nonviolence and truthfulness

- Detachment from worldly distractions

- Unwavering faith and trust in the divine

Such a person, Krishna says, is truly dear to him and is on the path to attaining eternal peace and liberation.

The Simplicity of Bhakti Yoga

Unlike other spiritual paths that require intense study, asceticism, or intellectual rigor, **Bhakti Yoga is based on sincerity and surrender**. Krishna states that anyone—regardless of background, caste, or social status—can attain him through pure devotion.

He reassures his devotees that even a simple offering of a leaf, a flower, or water—if given with love—is enough to reach him. This teaching highlights that what matters is not the material value of an offering, but the sincerity behind it.

The Path to Ultimate Liberation

Krishna concludes by urging Arjuna to dedicate all actions, thoughts, and emotions to him, assuring that those who surrender completely will attain him without fail. He explains that the highest form of devotion is one where the devotee asks for nothing, seeks nothing, and simply offers love unconditionally.

This chapter reinforces the idea that Bhakti is not just an emotional connection, but a transformative process. By constantly remembering Krishna, loving him selflessly, and embodying divine virtues, one transcends material existence and attains eternal union with the Supreme.

The Power of Pure Devotion

Chapter 12 of the *Bhagavad Gita* establishes Bhakti Yoga as the simplest, yet most profound path to liberation. Krishna reassures Arjuna that he is easily attainable through love and faith, and that those who embody devotion with humility and sincerity are dearest to him.

With this teaching, Krishna shifts the focus from intellectual pursuit and renunciation to the power of love and surrender, making spiritual realization accessible to all. This sets the stage for the deeper philosophical discussions that follow, where Krishna will reveal the relationship between the divine, the universe, and the eternal soul.

Arjuna said:

Those devotees who ever harmonised worship Thee, and those also who worship the Indestructible, the Unmanifested, whether of these is the more learned in yoga?(1)

The Blessed Lord said:

They who with mind[1] fixed on Me ever harmonised worship Me, with faith supreme endowed, these, in My opinion, are best in yoga.(2)

They who worship the Indestructible, the Ineffable, the unmanifested, Omnipresent, and Unthinkable, the Unchanging, Immutable, Eternal,(3)

Restraining and subduing the senses, regarding everything equally, in the welfare of all rejoicing, these also come unto Me.(4)

The difficulty of those whose minds are set on the Unmanifested is greater; for the path of the Unmanifested is hard for the embodied to reach.(5)

Those verily who, renouncing all actions in Me and intent on Me, worship meditating on Me, with whole-hearted yoga,(6)

These I speedily lift up from the ocean of death and existence, O Pârtha, their minds[2] being fixed on Me.(7)

Place thy mind[3] in me, into Me let thy Reason[4] enter; then without doubt thou shalt abide in Me hereafter.(8)

---

[1] Manah.
[2] Chetah.
[3] Manah.
[4] Buddhi.

90

And if thou art not able firmly to fix thy mind[5] on Me, then by the yoga of practice seek to reach Me, O Dhananjaya.(9)

If also thou art not equal to constant practice, be intent on My service; performing actions for My sake, thou shalt attain perfection.(10)

If even to do this thou hast not strength, then, taking refuge in union with Me, renounce all fruit of action with the self controlled.(11)

Better indeed is wisdom than constant-practice; than wisdom, meditation is better; than meditation, renunciation of the fruit of action; on renunciation follows peace.(12)

He who beareth no ill-will to any being, friendly and compassionate, without attachment and egoism, balanced in pleasure and pain, and forgiving,(13)

Ever content, harmonious, with the self-controlled, resolute, with mind[6] and Reason[7] dedicated to Me, he, My devotee, is dear to Me.(14)

He from whom the world doth not shrink away, who doth not shrink away from the world, freed from the anxieties of joy, anger, and fear, he is dear to me.(15)

He who wants nothing, is pure, expert, passionless, untroubled, renouncing every undertaking, he, My devotee, is dear to Me.(16)

He who neither loveth nor hateth, nor grieveth, nor desireth, renouncing good and evil, full of devotion, he is dear to Me.(17)

Alike to foe and friend, and also in fame and ignominy, alike in cold and heat, pleasures and pains, destitute of attachment,(18)

Taking equally praise and reproach, silent, wholly content with what cometh, homeless, firm in mind, full of devotion, that man is dear to Me.(19)

---

[5] Chitta.
[6] Manah.
[7] Buddhi.

They verily who partake of this life-giving wisdom[8] as taught herein, endued with faith, I their supreme Object, devotees, they are surpassingly dear to Me.(20)

Thus in the glorious Upanishads of the Bhagavad-Gita, the science of the Eternal, the scripture of Yoga, the dialogue between Shri Krishna and Arjuna, the twelfth discourse, entitled:

THE YOGA OF DEVOTION.

---

[8] Amrita-Dharma.

THIRTEENTH DISCOURSE

Understanding the Body and the Soul

Chapter 13 of the *Bhagavad Gita*, known as *Kshetra-Kshetragna Vibhaga Yoga* (The Yoga of the Field and the Knower of the Field), introduces one of the most profound philosophical discussions in the text. Krishna explains the distinction between **the body (Kshetra, the Field)** and **the soul (Kshetragna, the Knower of the Field)**, laying the foundation for understanding self-realization and spiritual wisdom.

Arjuna, seeking deeper insight into the nature of existence, asks Krishna to clarify what constitutes the body, the soul, knowledge, and the ultimate reality (Purusha and Prakriti). Krishna responds by outlining the relationship between the physical world, consciousness, and the Supreme Divine.

The Field (Kshetra) and the Knower of the Field (Kshetragna)

Krishna explains that the body is the Field (Kshetra), while the soul is the Knower of the Field (Kshetragna). The body represents matter and temporary existence, subject to change, decay, and death. The soul, however, is eternal, unchanging, and the observer of all experiences.

Beyond the individual soul, Krishna introduces the Supreme Knower—the Divine Consciousness that pervades all beings. He explains that while individual souls experience their respective bodies, Krishna himself is the Supreme Knower of all Fields, present within and beyond creation.

The Nature of Knowledge and Wisdom

Krishna then defines true knowledge, stating that wisdom is not merely intellectual understanding but the ability to distinguish between the eternal soul and the perishable body. He lists qualities that cultivate true wisdom, including:

- Humility and non-arrogance
- Detachment from material desires
- Patience and self-control

- Seeking solitude and inner contemplation

- Devotion to the Supreme and unwavering faith

Krishna emphasizes that real knowledge leads to liberation, while attachment to the material body leads to ignorance and suffering.

Purusha (Spirit) and Prakriti (Matter)

Expanding on these concepts, Krishna describes **Purusha (the eternal, conscious self)** and **Prakriti (the material world and nature)**. He explains that Prakriti is the source of all action, while Purusha remains the passive witness. The interaction between Purusha and Prakriti creates the illusion of the material world, binding souls to the cycle of birth and death.

Understanding this distinction allows one to transcend the physical realm and realize the eternal self.

The Supreme Reality: Krishna as the Ultimate Knower

Krishna asserts that beyond individual consciousness and material nature lies the Supreme Reality—himself. He is the universal consciousness that pervades all things, the creator, sustainer, and witness of existence.

He describes himself as:

- The light of all lights

- Beyond darkness and ignorance

- The ultimate object of knowledge

- The cause and essence of all beings

By meditating on Krishna as the Supreme Knower of all Fields, one attains liberation from illusion and unites with the Divine.

The Path to Liberation

Krishna explains that those who perceive the distinction between the Field and the Knower of the Field attain spiritual freedom. The enlightened person understands that the body is temporary, but the soul is eternal, leading to detachment from material suffering.

He emphasizes that one who realizes this truth is no longer bound by karma and transcends the illusion of individuality, merging with the infinite divine consciousness.

The Vision of True Knowledge

Chapter 13 deepens Arjuna's understanding of the relationship between the self, the body, and the Divine. Krishna teaches that true wisdom lies in recognizing:

- The body as the perishable Field

- The soul as the eternal Knower

- Krishna as the Supreme Consciousness pervading all existence

By cultivating this awareness, one transcends material illusion and attains self-realization and liberation. This sets the stage for the following chapters, where Krishna will further explain the influence of the Gunas (modes of nature) and the journey to spiritual freedom.

Arjuna said:

Matter and Spirit,[1] even the Field and the Knower of the Field, wisdom and that which ought to be known, these I fain would learn, O Keshava.(1)

The Blessed Lord said:

This body, son of Kuntî, is called the Field; that which knoweth it is called the Knower of the Field by the Sages.(2)

Understand Me as the Knower of the Field in all Fields, O Bhârata. Wisdom as to the Field and the Knower of the Field, that in My opinion is the wisdom.(3)

What that Field is and of what nature, how modified, and whence it is, and what He[2] is and what His powers, hear that now briefly from Me.(4)

---

[1] Prakriti and Purusha.
[2] Kshetrajña, the Knower of the Field.

Rishis have sung in manifold ways, in many various chants, and in decisive Brahma-sûtra verses[3] full of reasonings.(5)

The great Elements, Individuality[4], Reason[5], and also the unmanifested, the ten senses and the one, and the five pastures of the senses[6];(6)

Desire, aversion, pleasure, pain, combination[7], intelligence, firmness; these, briefly described, constitute the Field and its modifications.(7)

Humility, unpretentiousness, harmlessness, forgiveness, rectitude, service of the teacher, purity, steadfastness, self-control.(8)

Dispassion towards the objects of the senses, and also absence of egoism, insight into the pain and evil of birth, death, old age and sickness,(9)

Unattachment, absence of self-identification with son, wife or home, and constant balance of mind in wished-for and unwished-for events,(10)

Unflinching devotion to Me by yoga, without other objects, resort to sequestered places, absence of enjoyment in the company of men,(11)

Constancy in the wisdom of the Self,[8] understanding of the object of essential wisdom; that is declared to be the Wisdom; all against it is ignorance.(12)

I will declare that which ought to be known, that which being known immortality is enjoyed—the beginningless supreme Eternal, called neither being nor non-being.(13)

Everywhere That hath hands and feet, everywhere eyes, heads, and mouths; all-hearing, He dwelleth in the world, enveloping all,(14)

Shining with all sense-faculties without any senses; unattached supporting everything and free from qualities[9] enjoying qualities;[9] (15)

---

[3] Short terse sayings, concerning the Eternal.
[4] Ahañkara
[5] Buddhi.
[6] The five organs of knowledge, or senses, the five organs of action, the mind, and the object cognised by each of the five senses.
[7] The body.
[8] Adhyâtma; see vii, 29.
[9] Gunas.

Without and within all beings, immovable and also movable; by reason of His subtlety imperceptible; at hand and far away is That.(16)

Not divided amid beings, and yet seated distributively; that is to be known as the supporter of beings; He devours and He generates.(17)

That, the Light of all lights, is said to be beyond darkness; Wisdom, the Object of Wisdom, by Wisdom to be reached, seated in the hearts of all.(18)

Thus the Field, Wisdom and the Object of Wisdom, have been briefly told. My devotee, thus knowing, enters into My Being.(19)

Know thou that Matter[10] and Spirit[11] are both without beginning; and know thou also that modifications and qualities[12] are all Matter[10]-born.(20)

Matter[10] is called the cause of the generation of causes and effects; Spirit[11] is called the cause of the enjoyment of pleasure and pain.(21)

Spirit[11] seated in Matter[10] useth the qualities born of Matter[10]; attachment to the qualities[12] is the cause of his births in good and evil wombs.(22)

Supervisor and permitter, supporter, enjoyer, the great Lord, and also the supreme Self; thus is styled in this body the supreme Spirit.[10] (23)

He who thus knoweth Spirit[11] and Matter[10] with its qualities,[12] in whatsoever condition he may be, he shall not be born again.(24)

Some by meditation behold the Self in the self by the Self; others by the Sânkhya Yoga, and others by the Yoga of Action;(25)

Others also, ignorant of this, having heard of it from others, worship; and these also cross beyond death, adhering to what they had heard.(26)

Whatsoever creature is born immobile or mobile, know thou, O best of the Bhâratas, that it is from the union between the Field and the Knower of the Field.(27)

_____

[10] Prakriti.
[11] Purusha.
[12] Gunas.

Seated equally in all beings, the supreme Lord, unperishing within the perishing—he who thus seeth, he seeth.(28)

Seeing indeed everywhere the same Lord equally dwelling, he doth not destroy the Self, and thus treads the highest Path.(29)

He who seeth that Matter[10] verily performeth all actions, and that the Self is actionless, he seeth.(30)

When he perceiveth the diversified existence of beings as rooted in One, and spreading forth from it, then he reacheth the Eternal(31)

Being beginningless and without qualities[12], the imperishable supreme Self, though seated in the body, O Kaunteya, worketh not nor is affected.(32)

As the omnipresent ether is not affected, by reason of its subtlety, so seated everywhere in the body the Self is not affected.(33)

As the one sun illumineth the whole earth, so the Lord of the Field illumineth the whole Field, O Bhârata.(34)

They who by the eyes of Wisdom perceive this difference between the Field and the Knower of the Field, and the liberation of beings from Matter[13] they go to the Supreme.(35)

Thus in the glorious Upanishads of the Bhagavad-Gita, the science of the Eternal, the scripture of Yoga, the dialogue between Shrî Krishna and Arjuna, the thirteenth discourse entitled:

THE YOGA OF THE DISTINCTION BETWEEN THE FIELD AND THE KNOWER OF THE FIELD.

---

[13] Prakriti

FOURTEENTH DISCOURSE

The Influence of the Three Gunas

Chapter 14 of the *Bhagavad Gita*, known as *Guna-Traya-Vibhaga Yoga* (The Yoga of the Three Gunas), expands on the relationship between material nature (Prakriti) and spiritual consciousness. Krishna explains how the three Gunas (modes of nature)—Sattva (goodness), Rajas (passion), and Tamas (ignorance)—govern human behavior, thought, and spiritual evolution.

Krishna reveals that these Gunas bind the soul to the cycle of birth and death. However, by understanding them and transcending their influence, one can attain liberation (moksha) and unite with the Supreme Reality. This chapter is crucial because it teaches self-awareness, inner discipline, and detachment, allowing one to rise above material conditioning.

The Three Gunas and Their Effects

Krishna describes the three Gunas as the fundamental forces that shape existence:

1. **Sattva (Goodness):**

    o   Associated with light, wisdom, harmony, and purity.

    o   Brings peace, happiness, and clarity but can lead to attachment to knowledge and joy.

    o   Elevates the soul toward higher realms after death.

2. **Rajas (Passion):**

    o   Characterized by desire, restlessness, ambition, and action.

    o   Leads to attachment to work, competition, and material success.

    o   Binds the soul to the cycle of effort and repeated rebirths in active existence.

3. **Tamas (Ignorance):**

   o Linked to darkness, laziness, delusion, and lack of awareness.

   o Causes negligence, confusion, and inertia.

   o Leads the soul to lower births, ignorance, and suffering.

Krishna explains that every action, thought, and personality is influenced by a combination of these Gunas. However, only by transcending them can one attain true freedom.

How the Gunas Bind the Soul

Krishna emphasizes that Sattva binds through attachment to joy and knowledge, Rajas binds through attachment to action and achievement, and Tamas binds through attachment to ignorance and lethargy. While Sattva is the highest among the three, it still binds the soul to existence.

He teaches that one's spiritual journey is determined by which Guna predominates. At death:

- A **Sattvic person** reaches higher divine realms.

- A **Rajasic person** is reborn in active, striving conditions.

- A **Tamasic person** is reborn in lower, deluded states.

Rising Above the Gunas: The Path to Liberation

Krishna then presents the way to transcend the Gunas:

- **Through detachment and awareness**, one must observe these influences without being controlled by them.

- The **true seeker remains neutral**, neither chasing pleasure (Sattva), ambition (Rajas), nor sinking into delusion (Tamas).

- **By devotion to Krishna**, one moves beyond the Gunas and attains the eternal spiritual state.

Krishna declares that one who is beyond the Gunas becomes free from birth, death, old age, and suffering. Such a person reaches his supreme abode, never returning to the material world.

The Supreme Devotee: Transcending the Modes of Nature

Krishna concludes by describing the qualities of one who has transcended the Gunas:

- They remain undisturbed by pleasure, pain, success, and failure.

- They are detached from worldly actions, yet perform duties selflessly.

- They are devoted to Krishna, surrendering completely to his divine will.

By practicing Bhakti Yoga (devotion) and maintaining constant awareness, a seeker transcends material conditioning and attains spiritual freedom.

Mastering the Gunas to Attain Liberation

Chapter 14 provides a profound psychological and spiritual framework for understanding human nature. Krishna teaches that self-awareness, detachment, and devotion allow one to move beyond Sattva, Rajas, and Tamas, ultimately leading to liberation.

This chapter prepares Arjuna for deeper revelations on divine nature, karma, and dharma in the following discussions. It emphasizes that true freedom comes not by rejecting the world, but by rising above its influences through wisdom and devotion.

The Blessed Lord said:

I will again proclaim that supreme Wisdom, of all wisdom the best, which having known, all the Sages[1] have gone hence to the supreme Perfection.(1)

Having taken refuge in this Wisdom and being assimilated to My own nature, they are not re-born even in the emanation of a universe, nor are disquieted in the dissolution.(2)

My womb is the great Eternal; in that I place the germ; thence cometh the birth of all beings, O Bhârata.(3)

---

[1] Munis.

In whatsoever wombs mortals are produced, O Kaunteya, the great Eternal is their womb, I their generating father.(4)

Harmony,[2] Motion, Inertia, such are the qualities[3], Matter[4]-born; they bind fast in the body, O great-armed one, the indestructible dweller in the body.(5)

Of these Harmony from its stainlessness, luminous and healthy, bindeth by the attachment to bliss and the attachment to wisdom, O sinless one.(6)

Motion, the passion nature, know thou, is the source of attachment and thirst for life, O Kaunteya, that bindeth the dweller in the body by the attachment to action.(7)

But Inertia, know thou, born of unwisdom, is the deluder of all dwellers in the body; that bindeth by heedlessness, indolence and sloth, O Bharata.(8)

Harmony attacheth to bliss, Motion to action O Bharata. Inertia, verily, having shrouded wisdom, attacheth on the contrary to heedlessness.(9)

Now Harmony prevaileth, having overpowered Motion and Inertia, O Bhârata; now Motion, having overpowered Harmony and Inertia; and now Inertia, having overpowered Harmony and Motion.(10)

When the wisdom-light streameth forth from all the gates of the body, then it may be known that Harmony is increasing.(11)

Greed, outgoing energy, undertaking of actions, restlessness, desire—these are born of the increase of Motion, O best of the Bhâratas.(12)

Darkness, stagnation and heedlessness and also delusion—these are born of the increase of Inertia, O joy of the Kurus.(13)

If Harmony verily prevaileth when the embodied goeth to dissolution, then he goeth forth to the spotless worlds of the great Sages.(14)

Having gone to dissolution in Motion, he is born among those attached to action; if dissolved in Inertia, he is born in the wombs of the senseless.(15)

---

[2] More strictly Rhythm.
[3] Gunas.
[4] Prakriti.

It is said the fruit of a good action is harmonious and spotless; verily the fruit of Motion is pain, and the fruit of Inertia unwisdom(16)

From Harmony wisdom is born, and also greed from Motion; heedlessness and delusion are of Inertia and also unwisdom.(17)

They rise upwards who are settled in Harmony; the Active dwell in the midmost place: the Inert go downwards, enveloped in the vilest(18)

When the Seer perceiveth no agent other than the qualities[5], and knoweth That which is higher than the qualities,[5] he entereth into My Nature.(19)

When the dweller in the body hath crossed over these three qualities,[5] whence all bodies have been produced, liberated from birth, death, old age and sorrow, he drinketh the nectar of immortality[6].(20)

Arjuna said:

What are the marks of him who hath crossed over the three qualities[5], O Lord? How acteth he, and how doth he go beyond these three qualities[5]?(21)

The Blessed Lord said:

He, O Pândava, who hateth not radiance, nor outgoing energy, nor even delusion, when present, nor longeth after them, absent;(22)

He who, seated as a neutral, is unshaken by the qualities[5]; who, saying, "The qualities[5] revolve," standeth apart immovable.(23)

Balanced in pleasure and pain, self-reliant, to whom a lump of earth, a rock and gold are alike, the same to loved and unloved, firm, the same in censure and in praise,(24)

The same in honour and ignominy, the same to friend and foe, abandoning all undertakings—he is said to have crossed over the qualities.[5] (25)

And he who serveth Me exclusively by the Yoga of devotion, he, crossing beyond the qualities,[5] he is fit to become the Eternal.(26)

---

[5] Gunas.
[6] The Amrita.

For I am the abode of the Eternal, and of the indestructible nectar of immortality, of immemorial righteousness,[7] and of unending bliss.(27)

Thus in the glorious Upanishads of the Bhagavad-Gita, the science of the Eternal, the scripture of Yoga, the dialogue between Shri Krishna and Arjuna, the fourteenth discourse entitled:

THE YOGA OF SEPARATION FROM THE THREE QUALITIES.

---

[7] Dharma.

FIFTEENTH DISCOURSE

The Eternal and the Perishable

Chapter 15 of the *Bhagavad Gita*, known as *Purushottama Yoga* (The Yoga of the Supreme Person), presents one of the most profound metaphysical teachings in the text. Krishna describes the eternal and impermanent aspects of reality, using the symbol of the **Ashvattha tree (the cosmic tree of life)** to explain how souls remain bound to the material world. He then reveals how one can cut through illusion and reach the **Supreme Reality (Purushottama)**—Krishna himself.

This chapter shifts the focus toward understanding the nature of existence and the means to liberation. Krishna emphasizes that knowing the Supreme Person leads to ultimate freedom, transcending the cycle of birth and death.

The Inverted Tree: The Illusory Material World

Krishna begins with the analogy of the Ashvattha tree, describing it as an upside-down tree with roots above and branches below. This represents the material world, where:

- **The roots (Brahman)** connect to the divine source.

- **The branches (manifested world)** represent various desires, actions, and consequences.

- **The leaves (Vedic knowledge)** symbolize different spiritual paths and scriptures.

This tree binds souls to the material world, as people become attached to its branches (pleasures, ambitions, and karma). However, Krishna urges Arjuna to cut this tree down with the sword of detachment and seek the eternal root—his divine presence.

The Nature of the Supreme Person (Purushottama)

Krishna explains that there are three fundamental aspects of existence:

1. **The Perishable (Kshara Purusha)** – All material beings and objects that undergo birth and death.

2. **The Imperishable (Akshara Purusha)** – The eternal soul (Atman) that remains untouched by material changes.

3. **The Supreme Person (Purushottama)** – Krishna, the highest reality, who transcends both the perishable and imperishable and is the ultimate goal of all spiritual efforts.

This teaching clarifies that Krishna is beyond both the changing physical universe and the eternal soul—he is the source of both. Recognizing him as the Supreme Reality leads to liberation.

The Eternal Soul and Its Journey

Krishna further describes how the individual soul (Jivatma) moves from body to body, influenced by its karma and desires. He explains that:

- The ignorant do not perceive the soul's journey, but the wise recognize its eternal nature.

- Just as air carries scents, the soul carries impressions and experiences from one life to another.

- Only through self-realization and devotion can one break free from this cycle and return to the Supreme Person.

Krishna as the Ultimate Reality

Krishna declares that he is the sustaining force behind all existence:

- He is the light in the sun and moon.

- He is the fire in all beings.

- He is the intelligence of the wise and the strength of the strong.

- He is the essence of life and the source of remembrance and forgetfulness.

This reinforces the idea that Krishna is not separate from the world but is its inner essence, guiding all beings toward liberation.

The Path to Liberation: Devotion and Knowledge

Krishna explains that only those who recognize him as the Supreme Person (Purushottama) can attain true liberation. He urges Arjuna to cultivate:

- Detachment from worldly illusions.

- Self-knowledge to understand the eternal soul.

- Devotion (Bhakti) as the easiest and most direct path to reach him.

By surrendering to Krishna with love and faith, one transcends material bondage and reaches the eternal, divine state.

Attaining the Supreme Goal

Chapter 15 provides a clear and profound path to spiritual liberation, teaching that the material world is an illusion, but Krishna is the eternal reality beyond it. By cutting through attachment, recognizing Krishna as the Supreme Person, and surrendering in devotion, one escapes the endless cycle of birth and death.

This chapter sets the stage for Krishna's further revelations on divine knowledge, duty, and devotion, reinforcing that knowing and surrendering to Krishna is the highest wisdom.

The Blessed Lord said:

With roots above, branches below, the Asvattha is said to be indestructible; the leaves of it are hymns; he who knoweth it is a Veda-knower.(1)

Downwards and upwards spread the branches of it, nourished by the qualities[1]; the objects of the senses its buds; and its roots grow downwards, the bonds of action in the world of men.(2)

Nor here may be acquired knowledge of its form, nor its end, nor its origin, nor its rooting-place; this strongly rooted Asvattha having been cut down by the unswerving weapon of non-attachment,(3)

That path beyond may be sought, treading which there is no return. I go indeed to that Primal Man[2], whence the ancient energy forth-streamed.(4)

Without pride and delusion, victorious over the vice of attachment, dwelling constantly in the Self, desire pacified, liberated from the pairs of opposites known as pleasure and pain, they tread, undeluded, that indestructible path.(5)

---

[1] Gunas.
[2] Purusha.

Nor doth the sun lighten there, nor moon, nor fire; having gone thither they return not; that is My supreme abode.(6)

A portion of Mine own Self, transformed in the world of life into an immortal Spirit,[3] draweth round itself the senses of which the mind[4] is the sixth, veiled in matter[5].(7)

When the Lord acquireth a body and when He abandoneth it, He seizeth these[6] and goeth with them, as the wind takes fragrances from their retreats(8)

Enshrined in the ear, the eye, the touch, the taste and the smell, and in the mind[4] also, He enjoyeth the objects of the senses(9)

The deluded do not perceive (Him) when He departeth or stayeth or enjoyeth, swayed by the qualities[7]; the wisdom-eyed perceive.(10)

Yogîs also, struggling, perceive Him, established in the Self; but though struggling, the unintelligent perceive Him not, their selves untrained.(11)

That splendour issuing from the sun that enlighteneth the whole world, that which is in the moon and in fire, that splendour know as from Me.(12)

Permeating the soil, I support beings by my vital energy, and having become the delicious Soma[8] I nourish all plants.(13)

I, having become the Fire of Life[9], take possession of the bodies of breathing things, and united with the life-breaths[10], I digest the four kinds of food.(14)

And I am seated in the hearts of all, and from Me memory and wisdom and their absence. And that which is to be known in all the Vedas am I; and I indeed the Veda-knower and the author of the Vedanta.(15)

---

[3] Jîva, a life, individualised from the Universal Spirit.
[4] Manah.
[5] Prakriti.
[6] The senses and the mind.
[7] Gunas.
[8] "Having become the watery moon" is the accepted translation. Soma is a liquid, drawn from the Soma-plant. "Having become sap" is a probable translation.
[9] Vaisvânara.
[10] Prâna and Apâna.

There are two Energies[11] in this world, the destructible and the indestructible; the destructible is all beings, the unchanging is called the indestructible.(16)

The highest Energy[11] is verily Another, declared as the Supreme Self, He who, pervading all, sustaineth the three worlds, the indestructible Lord.(17)

Since I excel the destructible, and am more excellent also than the indestructible, in the world and in the Veda I am proclaimed the Supreme Spirit.[12] (18)

He who undeluded knoweth Me thus as the Supreme Spirit[12], he, all-knowing, worshippeth Me with his whole being, O Bhârata.(19)

Thus by Me this most secret teaching hath been told O sinless one. This known, he hath become illuminated and hath finished his work, O Bhârata.(20)

Thus in the glorious Upanishads of the Bhagavad-Gita, the science of the Eternal, the scripture of Yoga, the dialogue between Shrî Krishna and Arjuna, the fifteenth discourse, entitled:

THE YOGA OF ATTAINING THE SUPREME SPIRIT.

---

[11] Purusha.
[12] Purushottama, the highest Purusha.

SIXTEENTH DISCOURSE

The Two Paths of Human Nature

Chapter 16 of the *Bhagavad Gita*, known as *Daivasura Sampad Vibhaga Yoga* (The Yoga of the Divine and the Demonic), presents a sharp contrast between two types of human nature: **the divine (Daivi) and the demonic (Asuri)**. Krishna explains that individuals possess qualities that either lead them toward spiritual growth and liberation or keep them bound to ignorance and suffering.

This chapter serves as a moral and ethical guide, helping seekers recognize which traits to cultivate and which to overcome. Krishna emphasizes that divine qualities lead to self-realization and ultimate freedom, while demonic qualities cause bondage and suffering.

The Divine Qualities (Daivi Sampad)

Krishna describes the characteristics of those who are on the divine path, emphasizing virtues that lead to spiritual elevation. These include:

- **Fearlessness (Abhayam):** A state of inner security, knowing that Krishna protects and guides.

- **Purity of heart (Sattva Samshuddhi):** Freedom from deceit, selfishness, and ill intent.

- **Self-restraint (Dama):** Control over desires and emotions.

- **Compassion and truthfulness:** Acting with kindness, honesty, and integrity.

- **Nonviolence (Ahimsa):** Avoiding harm to any living being.

- **Detachment from material desires:** Living a life of simplicity and contentment.

Krishna assures Arjuna that those who embody these divine virtues are naturally inclined toward self-realization and liberation.

The Demonic Qualities (Asuri Sampad)

In contrast, Krishna warns against the characteristics of those with demonic tendencies, which keep the soul trapped in ego, illusion, and material suffering. These include:

- **Hypocrisy and arrogance:** A false sense of superiority and deception.

- **Harshness and cruelty:** Lack of compassion, acting with aggression and disregard for others.

- **Ignorance and delusion:** Rejecting spiritual wisdom and being blinded by worldly attachments.

- **Material obsession:** Seeking power, wealth, and pleasures without moral restraint.

- **Disregard for righteousness:** Ignoring dharma and acting selfishly.

Krishna states that those dominated by these qualities live in constant anxiety and dissatisfaction, ultimately leading to spiritual downfall.

The Consequences of These Paths

Krishna explains that divine individuals progress toward liberation, while those with demonic tendencies remain bound to the cycle of rebirth. He describes how ego, attachment, and material greed trap the soul in suffering, reinforcing that only through surrendering to Krishna and embracing divine virtues can one break free.

He warns that demoniac beings reject divine laws and act destructively, believing that the world is random and without moral order. Their ignorance leads them to further degradation, pushing them away from truth and toward greater suffering.

The Role of Free Will in Choosing One's Path

Krishna reassures Arjuna that spiritual progress is always possible. Even those with demonic qualities can change through self-discipline, wisdom, and devotion.

He emphasizes that the key to transformation is surrendering to the divine path, practicing virtues, and avoiding negative tendencies. Krishna reminds Arjuna that faith, humility, and devotion are the foundation of liberation.

The Importance of Scriptural Guidance

Krishna concludes by advising Arjuna that one should follow the guidance of sacred scriptures (Shastra) to discern right from wrong.

- Those who align their lives with divine teachings attain liberation.

- Those who reject spiritual wisdom remain lost in illusion.

Choosing the Path of Light

Chapter 16 serves as a moral and ethical guide, emphasizing that one's thoughts, words, and actions determine their spiritual fate. Krishna makes it clear that divine qualities lead to peace and ultimate freedom, while demonic tendencies lead to bondage and suffering.

By recognizing and cultivating virtues such as humility, self-control, and devotion, one aligns with Krishna's teachings and moves closer to liberation. This chapter reinforces the importance of self-awareness and conscious choices, preparing Arjuna for deeper revelations on spiritual wisdom and dharma in the following discourses.

———

The Blessed Lord said:

Fearlessness, cleanness of life, steadfastness in the Yoga of wisdom, almsgiving, self-restraint and sacrifice and study of the Scriptures, austerity and straightforwardness,(1)

Harmlessness, truth, absence of wrath, renunciation, peacefulness, absence of crookedness, compassion to living beings, uncovetousness, mildness, modesty, absence of fickleness,(2)

Vigour, forgiveness, fortitude, purity, absence of envy and pride—these are his who is born with the divine properties, O Bhârata.(3)

Hypocrisy, arrogance and conceit, wrath and also harshness and unwisdom are his who is born, O Pârtha, with demoniacal[1] properties.(4)

[1] Asuric; the Asuras were the enemies of the Suras or Gods.

The divine properties are deemed to be for liberation, the demoniacal for bondage. Grieve not, thou art born with divine properties, O Pândava.(5)

Twofold is the animal creation in this world, the divine and the demoniacal: the divine hath been described at length: hear from Me, O Pârtha, the demoniacal.(6)

Demoniacal men know neither right energy nor right abstinence; nor purity, nor even propriety, nor truth is in them.(7)

"The universe is without truth, without basis," they say, "without a God[2]; brought about by mutual union, and caused by lust and nothing else."(8)

Holding this view, these ruined selves of small understanding[3], of fierce deeds, come forth as enemies for the destruction of the world.(9)

Surrendering themselves to insatiable desires, possessed with vanity, conceit and arrogance, holding evil ideas through delusion, they engage in action with impure resolves.(10)

Giving themselves over to unmeasured thought whose end is death, regarding the gratification of desires as the highest, feeling sure that this is all,(11)

Held in bondage by a hundred ties of expectation, given over to lust and anger, they strive to obtain by unlawful means hoards of wealth for sensual enjoyments.(12)

"This to-day by me hath been won, that purpose I shall gain; this wealth is mine already, and also this shall be mine in future.(13)

"I have slain this enemy, and others also I shall slay. I am the Lord, I am the enjoyer, I am perfect, powerful, happy;(14)

"I am wealthy, well-born; what other is there that is like unto me? I will sacrifice, I will give alms, I will rejoice." Thus deluded by unwisdom,(15)

Bewildered by numerous thoughts, enmeshed in the web of delusion, addicted to the gratification of desire, they fall downwards into a foul hell.(16)

---

[2] Isvara; the ruler of a universe.
[3] Buddhi.

Self-glorifying, stubborn, filled with the pride and intoxication of wealth, they perform lip-sacrifices for ostentation, contrary to scriptural ordinance.(17)

Given over to egoism, power, insolence, lust and wrath, these malicious ones hate Me in the bodies of others and in their own.(18)

These haters, evil, pitiless, vilest among men in the world, I ever throw down into demoniacal wombs.(19)

Cast into demoniacal wombs, deluded birth after birth, attaining not to Me, O Kaunteya, they sink into the lowest depths.(20)

Triple is the gate of this hell, destructive of the self—lust, wrath, and greed; therefore let man renounce these three.(21)

A man liberated from these three gates of darkness, O son of Kunti, accomplisheth his own welfare, and thus reacheth the highest goal.(22)

He who, having cast aside the ordinances of the Scriptures, followeth the promptings of desire, attaineth not to perfection, nor happiness, nor the highest goal.(23)

Therefore let the Scriptures be thy authority, in determining what ought to be done, or what ought not to be done. Knowing what hath been declared by the ordinances of the Scriptures, thou oughtest to work in this world.(24)

Thus in the glorious Upanishads of the Bhagavad-Gita, the science of the Eternal, the scripture of Yoga, the dialogue between Shri Krishna and Arjuna, the sixteenth discourse, entitled:

THE YOGA OF DIVISION BETWEEN THE DIVINE AND THE DEMONIACAL.

SEVENTEENTH DISCOURSE

The Nature of Faith and Its Impact

Chapter 17 of the *Bhagavad Gita*, known as *Shraddha-Traya Vibhaga Yoga* (The Yoga of the Threefold Division of Faith), explores the nature of faith (Shraddha) and how it shapes human behavior and spiritual progress. Krishna explains that different kinds of faith arise from the influence of the three Gunas (modes of nature)—Sattva (goodness), Rajas (passion), and Tamas (ignorance).

Arjuna, still seeking clarity, asks Krishna about the faith of those who do not strictly follow scriptural teachings but still act with devotion. Krishna responds by revealing that faith is not uniform; it is shaped by an individual's inherent nature. He then categorizes faith, food, sacrifices, austerities, and charity according to the Gunas, showing how these aspects either elevate or degrade a person.

The Three Types of Faith

Krishna explains that faith determines a person's outlook on life, their worship, and their ultimate destination:

1. **Sattvic Faith (Faith in Purity and Truth)** – Those under the influence of Sattva worship divine beings, seek wisdom, and act with selflessness. Their faith is pure, uplifting, and in harmony with dharma.

2. **Rajasic Faith (Faith in Desire and Power)** – Those influenced by Rajas worship powerful spirits or worldly figures. Their faith is driven by ambition, ego, and material desires.

3. **Tamasic Faith (Faith in Darkness and Ignorance)** – Those dominated by Tamas engage in irrational or harmful rituals. Their faith is deluded, superstitious, and often destructive.

Krishna emphasizes that one's faith should align with truth and purity rather than blind attachment to personal inclinations.

The Influence of the Gunas on Food

Krishna further classifies food preferences based on the Gunas, explaining that diet affects physical health, mental clarity, and spiritual growth:

- **Sattvic food** – Fresh, wholesome, nourishing, and promotes longevity (fruits, vegetables, grains, dairy).

- **Rajasic food** – Overly spicy, bitter, or stimulating, leading to restlessness and excessive passion.

- **Tamasic food** – Stale, impure, or intoxicating, leading to ignorance and lethargy.

Through this, Krishna teaches that one's diet influences one's consciousness and overall spiritual disposition.

The Threefold Nature of Sacrifice, Austerity, and Charity

Krishna explains how sacrifice (Yajna), austerity (Tapas), and charity (Dana) can also be classified under the three Gunas:

1. **Sattvic Sacrifice,** Austerity, and Charity – Done with purity, devotion, and without expectation of reward.

2. **Rajasic Sacrifice,** Austerity, and Charity – Performed with selfish motives, seeking recognition and personal gain.

3. **Tamasic Sacrifice,** Austerity, and Charity – Done ignorantly, with improper intent, or causing harm.

Krishna emphasizes that only actions rooted in Sattva lead to true spiritual progress, while those in Rajas and Tamas keep the soul entangled in karma.

The Power of the Sacred Syllable 'OM'

Krishna highlights the importance of the sacred syllables OM, TAT, and SAT, which represent the eternal truth and divine reality. He explains that:

- **OM** – Represents the Supreme Reality and is chanted before all auspicious acts.

- **TAT** – Signifies selfless dedication, ensuring that all actions are done without ego.

- **SAT** – Symbolizes truth, purity, and eternal existence.

By invoking these sacred syllables, one sanctifies their actions and aligns them with divine will.

Choosing the Path of True Faith

Chapter 17 teaches that faith is not random—it is shaped by one's inner nature and choices. Krishna urges Arjuna to cultivate Sattvic faith, practice pure sacrifice, charity, and austerity, and align every action with truth and devotion.

By following this path, one transcends illusion, purifies the heart, and progresses toward ultimate liberation (moksha). This chapter reinforces the need for conscious living, where faith is refined and aligned with Krishna's divine guidance.

————

Arjuna said:

Those that sacrifice full of faith,[1] but casting aside the ordinances of the Scriptures, what is verily their condition, O Krishna? Is it one of Purity, Passion, or Darkness[2]?(1)

The Blessed Lord said:

Threefold is by nature the inborn faith of the embodied—pure, passionate, and dark. Hear thou of these.(2)

The faith of each is shaped to his own nature, O Bhârata. The man consists of his faith[3]; that which his faith is, he is even that.(3)

Pure men worship the Gods; the passionate the gnomes and giants[4]; the others, the dark folk, worship ghosts and troops of nature-spirits[5].(4)

---

[1] Shraddhâ.

[2] The three qualities, Sattva, Rajah, Tamah, are here used in their moral correspondences, and are therefore translated as Purity, Passion, and Darkness

[3] That is, the man's faith shows what is the man's character.

[4] Yakshas, gnomes, are the servants of the Lord of Wealth, *i. e.*, are connected with metals; Râkshasas, giants, or Titans, are the gigantic inhabitants of Atlantis versed in magic and sorcery.

[5] Pretas, ghosts, are departed men; while Bhûtas, nature-spirits, are of a somewhat goblin-like type.

The men who perform severe austerities, unenjoined by the Scriptures, wedded to vanity and egoism, impelled by the force of their desires and passions,(5)

Unintelligent, tormenting the aggregated elements forming the body, and Me also, seated in the inner body, know these demoniacal in their resolves.(6)

The food also which is dear to each is threefold, as also sacrifice, austerity and almsgiving. Hear thou the distinction of these.(7)

The foods that augment vitality, energy, vigour, health, joy and cheerfulness, delicious, bland, substantial and agreeable, are dear to the pure.(8)

The passionate desire foods that are bitter, sour, saline, over-hot, pungent, dry and burning and which produce pain, grief and sickness.(9)

That which is stale and flat, putrid and corrupt, leavings also and unclean, is the food dear to the dark.(10)

The sacrifice which is offered by men without desire for fruit, as enjoined by the ordinances, under the firm belief that sacrifice is a duty, that is pure.(11)

The sacrifice offered with a view verily to fruit, and also indeed for self-glorification, O best of the Bhâratas; know thou that to be of passion.(12)

The sacrifice contrary to the ordinances, without distributing food, devoid of words of power[6] and without gifts[7], empty of faith, is said to be of darkness.(13)

Worship given to the Gods, to the twice-born, to the teachers[8] and to the wise, purity, straightforwardness, continence and harmlessness, are called the austerity of the body.(14)

Speech causing no annoyance, truthful, pleasant and beneficial, the practice of the study of the Scriptures, are called the austerity of speech.(15)

---

[6] Mantras.
[7] To the officiating priests.
[8] Gurus.

Mental happiness, equilibrium, silence, self-control, purity of nature—these are called the austerity of the mind[9].(16)

This threefold austerity, performed by men with the utmost faith, without desire for fruit, harmonised, is said to be pure.(17)

The austerity which is practised with the object of gaining respect, honour and worship, and for ostentation, is said to be of passion, unstable and fleeting.(18)

That austerity done under a deluded understanding, with self-torture, or with the object of destroying another, that is declared of darkness.(20)

That alms given to one who does nothing in return, believing that a gift ought to be made in a fit place and time to a worthy person, that alms is accounted pure.(20)

That given with a view to receiving in return, or looking for fruit again, or grudgingly, that alms is accounted of passion.(21)

That alms given at unfit place and time, and to unworthy persons, disrespectfully and contemptuously, that is declared of darkness.(22)

"Aum Tat Sat," this has been considered to be the threefold designation of the Eternal. By that were ordained of old Brâhmanas, Vedas and sacrifices.(23)

Therefore with the pronunciation of "Aum" the acts of sacrifice, gift and austerity as laid down in the ordinances are always commenced by the knowers of the Eternal.(24)

With the pronunciation of "Tat" and without aiming at fruit are performed the various acts of sacrifice, austerity and gift, by those desiring liberation.(25)

"Sat" is used in the sense of reality and goodness; likewise, O Pârtha, the word "Sat" is used in the sense of a good work.(26)

Steadfastness in sacrifice, austerity and gift is also called "Sat", and action for the sake of the Supreme[10] is also named "Sat."(27)

---

[9] Manah.
[10] Tat

Whatsoever is wrought without faith, oblation, gift, austerity, or other deed, "Asat" it is called, O Pârtha; it is nought, here or hereafter.(28)

Thus in the glorious Upanishads of the Bhagavad-Gita, the science of the Eternal, the scripture of Yoga, the dialogue between Shrî Krishna and Arjuna, the seventeenth discourse, entitled:

THE YOGA OF THE DIVISION OF THREEFOLD FAITH.

EIGHTEENTH DISCOURSE

The Final Teachings on Renunciation and Liberation

Chapter 18 of the *Bhagavad Gita*, known as *Moksha-Sannyasa Yoga* (The Yoga of Liberation Through Renunciation), is the longest and most comprehensive chapter. Here, Krishna summarizes and clarifies the core teachings of the entire Gita, emphasizing the nature of renunciation (Sannyasa), the significance of duty (Dharma), and the supreme path of devotion (Bhakti Yoga).

Arjuna, still grappling with doubts, asks Krishna to explain the true meaning of renunciation—whether one should give up all action or simply renounce attachment to results. Krishna resolves this by explaining the difference between Sannyasa (renouncing selfish desires) and Tyaga (renouncing attachment to results while continuing duty). He then reinforces that devotion to him is the highest means to liberation.

The Threefold Nature of Renunciation

Krishna describes three kinds of renunciation based on the three Gunas:

1. **Sattvic Renunciation (Pure Renunciation)** – Performing duty without attachment to rewards and dedicating all actions to the divine.

2. **Rajasic Renunciation (Passionate Renunciation)** – Abandoning duties due to discomfort, fear, or attachment to personal gain.

3. **Tamasic Renunciation (Ignorant Renunciation)** – Avoiding responsibilities out of laziness, ignorance, or misunderstanding.

Krishna teaches that true renunciation is not the rejection of action, but the abandonment of selfish motives and ego. Those who perform duty with detachment and surrender attain purity of mind and ultimate liberation.

The Five Causes of Action and the Role of the Self

Krishna explains that every action consists of **five factors**:

1. **The body** (the instrument of action)

2. **The doer** (the individual performing the act)

3. **The senses** (which facilitate perception and interaction)

4. **The mind** (which influences decision-making)

5. **The divine will** (which ultimately governs all results)

Understanding this, Krishna clarifies that the enlightened person does not develop egoistic pride over achievements, realizing that all actions arise from divine forces. The wise recognize that they are not the true doers and thus remain unaffected by karma.

The Threefold Division of Duty (Dharma)

Krishna further classifies duty and action based on the Gunas:

- **Sattvic action – Performed selflessly and in harmony with dharma.**

- **Rajasic action** – Driven by personal ambition and attachment to rewards.

- **Tamasic action** – Done without thought, morality, or discipline.

He reinforces that everyone is bound by their inherent nature (Svadharma) and that fulfilling one's duty without attachment leads to liberation.

The Fourfold Division of Society

Krishna explains the Varna system (fourfold classification of human roles), emphasizing that it is based on qualities (Gunas) and actions (karma), not birth:

1. **Brahmins (intellectuals and teachers)** – Representing wisdom and purity.

2. **Kshatriyas (warriors and rulers)** – Governed by strength and leadership.

3. **Vaishyas (merchants and agriculturists)** – Focused on trade and productivity.

4. **Shudras (service workers)** – Providing essential labor and support.

Krishna clarifies that all roles are equally important and that fulfilling one's designated duty with devotion is a path to spiritual perfection.

The Ultimate Path: Bhakti Yoga and Surrender to Krishna

As the Gita reaches its climax, Krishna declares complete surrender (Sharanagati) to him as the highest path:

"Abandon all forms of duty and surrender to me alone. I shall free you from all sins. Do not fear."

This verse marks the culmination of all teachings, reinforcing that Bhakti (devotion) is superior to mere knowledge, action, or renunciation. By surrendering to Krishna, one is liberated from all karmic bondage.

Arjuna's Final Decision

After receiving Krishna's wisdom, Arjuna finally overcomes doubt and resolves to fight, embracing his duty as a warrior with complete faith.

Chapter 18 serves as the ultimate synthesis of all paths—Karma Yoga (selfless action), Jnana Yoga (knowledge), and Bhakti Yoga (devotion)—emphasizing that devotion to Krishna is the supreme means to liberation. This concluding discourse solidifies the Gita's timeless message: through righteousness, detachment, and surrender, one attains eternal peace and divine union.

Arjuna said:

I desire, O mighty-armed, to know severally the essence of renunciation,[1] O Hrishîkesha, and of relinquishment[2], O Keshinishûdana[3].(1)

The Blessed Lord said:

Sages have known as renunciation the renouncing of works with desire; the relinquishing of the fruit of all actions is called relinquishment by the wise.(2)

---

[1] Sannyâsa.
[2] Tyâga.
[3] Slayer of Keshi, a demon.

"Action should be relinquished as an evil,"[4] declare some thoughtful men; "acts of sacrifice, gift and austerity should not be relinquished," say others.(3)

Hear my conclusions as to that relinquishment, O best of the Bhâratas; since relinquishment, O tiger of men, has been explained as threefold.(4)

Acts of sacrifice, gift and austerity should not be relinquished, but should be performed; sacrifice, gift and also austerity are the purifiers of the intelligent.(5)

But even these actions should be done leaving aside attachment and fruit, O Pârtha; that is my certain and best belief.(6)

Verily renunciation of actions that are prescribed is not proper; the relinquishment thereof from delusion is said to be of darkness.(7)

He who relinquisheth an action from fear of physical suffering, saying "Painful," thus performing a passionate relinquishment, obtaineth not the fruit of relinquishment.(8)

He who performeth a prescribed action, saying, "it ought to be done," O Arjuna, relinquishing attachment and also fruit, that relinquishment is regarded as pure.(9)

The relinquisher pervaded by purity, intelligent and with doubts cut away, hateth not unpleasurable action nor is attached to pleasurable.(10)

Nor indeed can embodied beings completely relinquish action; verily he who relinquisheth the fruit of action, he is said to be a relinquisher.(11)

Good, evil and mixed—threefold is the fruit of action hereafter for the non-relinquisher; but there is none ever for the renouncer.(12)

These five causes, O mighty-armed, learn of Me as declared in the Sâñkhya system for the accomplishment of all actions:(13)

The body, the actor, the various organs, the diverse kinds of energies, and the presiding deities also, the fifth.(15)

---

[4] Some read: "Because it is evil."

Whatever action a man performeth by his body, speech and mind,[5] whether right or the reverse, these five are the cause thereof.(15)

That being so, he verily who—owing to untrained Reason[6]—looketh on his Self, which is isolated, as the actor, he of perverted intelligence, seeth not.(16)

He who is free from the egoistic notion, whose Reason[6] is not affected, though he slay these peoples, he slayeth not, nor is bound.(17)

Knowledge, the knowable and the knower, the threefold impulse to action; the organ, the action, the actor, the threefold constituents of action.(18)

Knowledge, action and actor in the category of qualities[7] are also said to be severally threefold, from the difference of qualities**Errore. Il segnalibro non è definito.**; hear thou duly these also.(19)

That by which one indestructible Being is seen in all beings, inseparate in the separated, know thou that knowledge as pure.(20)

But that knowledge which regardeth the several manifold existences in all beings as separate, that knowledge know thou as of passion;(21)

While that which clingeth to each one thing as if it were the whole, without reason, without grasping the reality, narrow, that is declared to be dark.(22)

An action which is ordained, done by one undesirous of fruit, devoid of attachment, without love or hate, that is called pure.(23)

But that action that is done by one longing for desires, or again with egoism, or with much effort, that is declared to be passionate.(24)

The action undertaken from delusion, without regard to capacity and consequences—loss and injury to others—that is declared to be dark.(25)

Liberated from attachment, not egoistic, endued with firmness and confidence, unchanged by success or failure, that actor is called pure.(26)

_____

[5] Manah.
[6] Buddhi.
[7] Gunas.

Impassioned, desiring to obtain the fruit of actions, greedy, harmful, impure, moved by joy and sorrow, such an actor is pronounced passionate.(27)

Discordant, vulgar, stubborn, cheating, malicious, indolent, despairful, procrastinating, that actor is called dark.(28)

The division of Reason[8] and of firmness also, threefold according to the qualities[9], hear thou related, unreservedly and severally, O Dhananjaya.(29)

That which knoweth energy and abstinence, what ought to be done and what ought not to be done, fear and fearlessness, bondage and liberation, that Reason[8] is pure, O Pârtha.(30)

That by which one understandeth away Right and Wrong[10] and also what ought to be done and what ought not to be done, that Reason,[11] O Pârtha, is passionate.(31)

That which, enwrapped in darkness, thinketh wrong[12] to be right[13] and seeth all things subverted, that Reason[11], O Pârtha, is of darkness.32)

The unwavering firmness by which, through Yoga, one restraineth the activity of the mind[14], of the life breaths and of the sense-organs, that firmness, O Pârtha, is pure.(33)

But the firmness, O Arjuna, by which, from attachment desirous of fruit, one holdeth fast duty[15], desire and wealth, that firmness, O Pârtha, is passionate.(34)

That by which one from stupidity doth not abandon sleep, fear, grief, despair, and also vanity, that firmness, O Pârtha, is dark.(35)

---

[8] Buddhi.
[9] Gunas.
[10] Dharma and Adharma, Right and Wrong in the widest sense, law and lawlessness.
[11] Buddhi.
[12] Adharma.
[13] Dharma.
[14] Manah.
[15] Dharma.

And now the threefold kinds of pleasure hear thou from Me, O bull of the Bhâratas. That in which one by practice rejoiceth, and which putteth an end to pain;(36)

Which at first is as venom but in the end is as nectar; that pleasure is said to be pure, born of the blissful knowledge of the Self.(37)

That which from the union of the senses with their objects at first is as nectar, but in the end is like venom, that pleasure is accounted passionate.(38)

That pleasure which both at first and afterwards is delusive of the self, arising from sleep, indolence and heedlessness, that is declared dark.(39)

There is not an entity, either on the earth or again in heaven among the Shining Ones, that is liberated from these three qualities,[16] born of Matter[17].(40)

Of Brâhmanas, Kshattriyas, Vaishyas and Shûdras, O Parantapa, the duties[18] have been distributed, according to the qualities[16] born of their own natures.(41)

Serenity, self-restraint, austerity, purity, forgiveness and also uprightness, wisdom, knowledge, belief in God, are the Brâhmana duty[19], born of his own nature.(42)

Prowess, splendour, firmness, dexterity, and also not flying from battle, generosity, the nature of a ruler, are the Kshattriya duty[19], born of his own nature.(43)

Ploughing, protection of kine, and trade are the Vaishya duty[19], born of his own nature. Action of the nature of service is the Shûdra duty,[19] born of his own nature.(44)

Man reacheth perfection by each being intent on his own duty[19]. Listen thou how perfection is won by him who is intent on his own duty[19].(45)

---

[16] Gunas.

[17] Prakriti.

[18] Karma; it is action arising from the nature fashioned by past thoughts and desires.

[19] Karma.

He from whom is the emanation of beings, by Whom all This is pervaded, by worshipping Him in his own duty[19] a man winneth perfection.(46)

Better is one's own duty[20] though destitute of merits than the well-executed duty[20] of another. He who doeth the duty[19] laid down by his own nature incurreth not sin.(47)

Congenital duty[19], O son of Kunti, though defective, ought not to be abandoned. All undertakings indeed are clouded by defects as fire by smoke.(48)

He whose Reason[21] is everywhere unattached, the self-subdued, dead to desires, he goeth by renunciation to the supreme perfection of freedom from obligation.[19] (49)

How he who hath attained perfection obtaineth the Eternal, that highest state of wisdom, learn thou from Me only succinctly, O Kaunteya.(50)

United to this Reason,[21] purified, controlling the self by firmness, having abandoned sound and the other objects of the senses, having laid aside passion and malice,(51)

Dwelling in solitude, abstemious, speech, body and mind[22] subdued, constantly fixed in meditation and yoga[23], taking refuge in dispassion,(52)

Having cast aside egoism, violence, arrogance, desire, wrath, covetousness, selfless and peaceful—he is fit to become the Eternal.(53)

Becoming the Eternal, serene in the Self, he neither grieveth nor desireth; the same to all beings, he obtaineth supreme devotion unto Me.(54)

By devotion he knoweth Me in essence, who and what I am; having thus known Me in essence he forthwith entereth into the Supreme.[24] (55)

Though ever performing all actions, taking refuge in Me, by My grace he obtaineth the eternal indestructible abode.(56)

---

[20] Dharma. There is a subtle difference in these words, here used almost interchangeably. Karma arises from the past; Dharma also so arises, but implies also the law by which the next step in evolution is made.
[21] Buddhi.
[22] Manah.
[23] Some read "dhyânayoga", Yoga of "meditation."
[24] That.

Renouncing mentally all works in Me, intent on Me, resorting to the yoga of discrimination[25], have thy thought ever on Me.(57)

Thinking on Me, thou shalt overcome all obstacles by My grace: but if from egoism thou wilt not listen, thou shalt be destroyed utterly.(58)

Entrenched in egoism, thou thinkest, "I will not fight;" to no purpose thy determination; nature will constrain thee.(59)

O son of Kuntî, bound by thine own duty[26] born of thine own nature, that which from delusion thou desirest not to do, even that helplessly thou shalt perform.(60)

The Lord dwelleth in the hearts of all beings, O Arjuna, by His illusive Power[27] causing all beings to revolve, as though mounted on a potter's wheel.(61)

Flee unto Him for shelter with all thy being, O Bhârata; by His grace thou shalt obtain supreme peace, the everlasting dwelling-place.(62)

Thus hath wisdom, more secret than secrecy itself, been declared unto thee by Me; having reflected on it fully, then act thou as thou listest.(63)

Listen thou again to My supreme word, most secret of all; beloved art thou of Me, and steadfast of heart, therefore will I speak for thy benefit.(64)

Merge thy mind[28] in Me, be my devotee, sacrifice to Me, prostrate thyself before Me, thou shalt come even to Me. I pledge thee My troth; thou art dear to Me.(65)

Abandoning all duties[29] come unto Me alone for shelter; sorrow not, I will liberate thee from all sins.(66)

Never is this to be spoken by thee to anyone who is without asceticism, nor without devotion, nor to one who desireth not to listen, nor yet to him who speaketh evil of Me.(67)

---

[25] Buddhi-yoga.
[26] Karma.
[27] Mâyâ.
[28] Manah.
[29] Dharmas.

He who shall declare this supreme secret among My devotees, having shown the highest devotion for Me, without doubt he shall come to Me.[30] (68)

Nor is there any among men who performeth dearer service to Me than he, nor any other shall be more beloved by Me on earth than he.(69)

And he who shall study this sacred dialogue of ours, by him I shall be worshipped with the sacrifice of wisdom. Such is My mind.(70)

The man also who, full of faith, merely heareth it unreviling, even he, freed from evil, obtaineth the radiant worlds of the righteous.(71)

Hath this been heard, O son of Prithâ, with one-pointed mind? Has thy delusion, caused by unwisdom, been destroyed, O Dhananjaya?(72)

Arjuna said:

Destroyed is my delusion. I have gained knowledge[31] through Thy grace, O Immutable one. I am firm, my doubts have fled away. I will do according to Thy word.(73)

Sanjaya said:

I heard this marvellous dialogue of Vâsudeva, and of the great-souled Partha, causing my hair to stand on end.(74)

By the favour of Vyâsa I listened to this secret and supreme yoga from the Lord of Yoga, Krishna Himself, speaking before mine eyes.(75)

O King, remembering, remembering this marvellous and holy dialogue between Keshava and Arjuna, I rejoice again and again.(76)

Remembering, remembering, also that most marvellous form of Hari, great is my wonder, O King. I rejoice, again and again.(77)

Wherever is Krishna, Yoga's Lord, wherever is Pârtha, the archer, assured are there prosperity, victory and happiness. So I think.[32] (78)

---

[30] Some read "asamsayah," which would mean "being freed from doubts."
[31] Literally "memory".
[32] Shri Shankaracharya's reading would run, translated: "There is prosperity, victory, happiness, and firm morality."

Thus in the glorious Upanishads of the Bhagavad-Gita, the science of the Eternal, the scripture of Yoga, the dialogue between Shrî Krishna and Arjuna, the eighteenth discourse, entitled:

THE YOGA OF LIBERATION BY RENUNCIATION.

Thus the Bhagavad-Gita hath ending.

Peace be to all Worlds.

Printed in Dunstable, United Kingdom

65685573R00077

1

Table of Contents

Introduction

Diverticula of the colon are common in older people. They commonly cause no symptoms, and in most cases no treatment is needed. However, a high-fibre diet is usually advised to help prevent complications. In some cases, diverticula cause pain and other symptoms. Sometimes a diverticulum may bleed and cause a sudden, painless bleed from the back passage (anus), which can be heavy. In some cases, one or more diverticula become infected to cause diverticulitis. This can cause severe tummy (abdominal) pain and high temperature (fever). A course of medicines called antibiotics may be required. Complications caused by diverticulitis such as a collection of pus (abscess) or a perforated bowel - are uncommon, but are serious.

A diverticulum is a small pouch with a narrow neck that sticks out from (protrudes from) the wall of the gut (intestine). 'Diverticula' means more than one diverticulum. They can develop on any part of the gut but usually occur in the colon (sometimes called the large bowel or large intestine). They most commonly develop in the section of the colon leading towards the back passage (rectum). This is where the stools (faeces) are becoming more solid. This is on the left-hand side of the tummy (abdomen). Several diverticula may develop over time. Some people eventually develop many diverticula.

Diverticula are pouches that form in the intestinal mucosa. The interior wall of the affected area of the intestine bulges outward through the intestinal muscles. Typically, this causes small balloon-shaped bulges in the intestine. Stool can accumulate in them.

Diverticula in the intestine are often harmless but can lead to symptoms and pain.

Simply put, there are three types:

- Diverticulosis: the interior wall of the intestine bulges outward in several places. The bulges do not cause symptoms.
- Diverticular disease: the bulges lead to symptoms or complications.
- Diverticulitis: the bulges are inflamed.

Diverticula can lead to recurring or long-term symptoms. In this case, it is called chronic diverticular disease. Generally speaking, diverticulitis can be treated successfully. However, there can be serious consequences if the inflammation spreads.

How are diverticula noticed?

Diverticula seldom cause problems.

Most diverticula do not cause symptoms. Diverticular disease often causes pain in the left abdomen while very rarely in the right. Typical indications are bloating, constipation, or diarrhea. Symptoms are often temporary, but can persist. In many cases, the symptoms become more intense after eating and then improve after a bowel movement. Diverticula can sometimes also bleed.

Diverticulitis (intestinal disease): woman sitting on the toilet holding a roll of toilet paper in her hand.

Diverticulitis often causes sudden, dull pain in the abdomen. This can be accompanied by a slight fever. Other symptoms include constipation, diarrhea, bloating, nausea, and sometimes cramps. Vomiting is less common. When the doctor presses on the stomach during an examination, the stomach muscles tighten reflexively; this is known as muscular defense. When released suddenly, the pain increases.

Risk factors for diverticulitis are age, weak connective tissue, bowel movement disorders, a genetic risk and being overweight.

Diverticula form in areas where there are weak intestinal muscles. Typically, they appear in the S-form part of the lower intestine known as the sigmoid colon. In this 40 to 45-cm long region above the rectum, pressure caused by the stool pressing against the interior wall of the intestine is the greatest.

Some people are more susceptible to diverticula for genetic reasons. Diverticulosis occurs more often in older or obese people. Further risk factors include weak connective tissue and impaired bowel movements. The impact of lifestyle on the disease is still unclear.

Evidence indicates that a diet low in fiber can increase the risk of diverticular disease, because this type of diet can cause constipation and a hard bowel movement. Other possible factors are a diet with too much red meat, smoking, and a lack of exercise.

The reason for the presence of diverticula in some people and not in others is still unknown, as is what increases the risk of contracting the disease. One possible factor is poor circulation and formation of hard feces particles in the diverticula.

What are the symptoms and problems caused by diverticula?

It is common for no symptoms to develop called diverticulosis

In about 3 in 4 people who develop diverticula, the diverticula cause no harm or symptoms. The term diverticulosis means that diverticula are present, but do not cause any symptoms or problems. In most cases, the condition will not be known about as there are no symptoms. Sometimes diverticula are discovered as an incidental finding if you are having tests such as colonoscopy or barium enema for other reasons.

Diverticular disease

This term is used when diverticula cause intermittent, lower tummy (abdominal) pain or bloating (without swelling (inflammation) or infection - discussed later). The pain is usually crampy and tends to come and go. The pain is most commonly in the lower left part of the tummy (abdomen). You may get ease from pain and bloating by going to the toilet to pass stools (faeces). Some people develop diarrhoea or constipation, and some people pass mucus with their stools. It is not clear how diverticula cause these symptoms.

Symptoms of diverticular disease can be similar to those that occur with a condition called irritable bowel syndrome (IBS). However, IBS usually affects younger adults. So, symptoms that first develop in a younger adult are more likely to be due to IBS and symptoms that first develop in older people are more likely to be due to diverticular disease. However, in some cases it is difficult to tell if symptoms are due to diverticular disease or to IBS.

A diagnosis of diverticular disease is usually made by confirming the presence of diverticula and by ruling out other causes of the symptoms. Note: the symptoms of diverticular disease, especially if they start in an older person, can also be similar to those of early bowel cancer. Therefore, tell a doctor if you develop these symptoms, as some tests may need to be arranged. For example, a test called colonoscopy may be advised. To carry out this test, a doctor uses a special flexible telescope to look into the bowel. This can confirm the presence of diverticula, and rule out bowel cancer.

Diverticulitis (infection)

Diverticulitis is a condition where one or more of the diverticula become inflamed and infected. This may occur if some faeces get trapped and stagnate in a diverticulum. Germs (bacteria) in the trapped faeces may then multiply and cause infection. About 1 in 5 people with diverticula develop a bout of diverticulitis at some stage. Some people have recurring bouts of diverticulitis. Symptoms of diverticulitis include:

A constant pain in the abdomen. It is most commonly in the lower left side of the abdomen, but can occur in any part of the abdomen. Indeed, in people of Asian origin, it sometimes occurs on the right side.

- High temperature (fever).
- Constipation or diarrhoea.
- Some blood mixed with your stools.

- Feeling sick (nauseated) or being sick (vomiting).
- Obstruction, abscess, fistula, and peritonitis

An infected diverticulum (diverticulitis) sometimes gets worse and causes complications. Possible complications include:

- A blockage (obstruction) of the colon.
- A collection of pus (abscess) that may form in the abdomen.
- A channel (fistula) that may form to other organs such as the bladder.
- A hole (perforation) in the wall of the bowel that can lead to infection inside the abdomen (peritonitis).

Surgery is usually needed to treat these serious but uncommon complications.

Bleeding

A diverticulum may occasionally bleed and you may pass some blood via your back passage (anus). The bleeding is usually abrupt and painless. The bleeding is due to a burst blood vessel that sometimes occurs in the wall of a diverticulum and so the amount of blood loss can be heavy. A very large bleed requiring an emergency blood transfusion occurs in some cases. However, the bleeding stops on its own in about 3 in 4 cases. Sometimes an operation is needed to stop the bleeding. Sometimes just a slight bleed occurs.

Note: always report bleeding from the bowel (via your anus) to a doctor. You should not assume bleeding is from a diverticulum. Other more serious conditions such as bowel cancer need to be ruled out.

As diverticulosis means diverticula with no symptoms, there is no need for any treatment.

However, a high-fibre diet is usually advised. A high-fibre diet is generally considered a good thing for everyone anyway - whether you have diverticula or not. Adults should aim to eat between 18 and 30 grams of fibre per day. Fibre helps to make larger and softer stools (faeces) and helps to prevent constipation. Also, a high-fibre diet may prevent further diverticula from forming. This may reduce the risk of developing problems in the future with diverticula, such as diverticulitis. See the next section for more details of a high-fibre diet.

There is evidence that you may reduce your risk of developing symptoms if you:

- Stop smoking
- Exercise
- Lose weight if you are overweight or obese

What is the treatment for diverticular disease?

Diverticulosis diet

A high-fibre diet is usually advised as it helps to keep stools (faeces) soft and bulky and reduces pressure on the colon. It can ease pain, bloating, constipation and diarrhoea and prevents hard stools becoming lodged within the pouches. It can also help to prevent the formation of further diverticula, which may reduce the risk of the condition getting any worse.

We need about 18 g of fibre each day, which should come from a variety of high-fibre foods. You may have symptoms of wind and bloating if you suddenly increase the amount of fibre you eat. Any increase should be gradual to prevent this, and to allow your gut (intestine) to become used to the extra fibre. A useful guide is to make one change every few days. For example, start by swapping white bread for wholemeal bread. Introduce something new every few days, such as adding beans or extra vegetables to a casserole or Bolognese, or having a piece of fruit for pudding.

High-fibre foods to include:

- Whole grains, fruit and vegetables.
- Wholemeal or wholewheat bread and flour (for baking).
- Wholegrain breakfast cereals such as All-Bran®, Weetabix®, muesli, etc.
- Brown rice and wholewheat pasta.
- Wheat bran.
- Beans, pulses and legumes.

Meeting the government recommendation of eating at least five fruit and vegetable portions each day will make sure that you are well on your way to getting plenty of fibre. A portion is about 80 g or what roughly fits in the palm of your hand. Apples, pears, oranges, blueberries, strawberries, broccoli, asparagus and dried figs are all excellent fibre sources.

Fibre supplements may be advised if a high-fibre diet does not ease symptoms. Several types are available at pharmacies, health food shops, or on prescription. A pharmacist will advise you. Although the effects of fibre supplements to ease symptoms may be seen in a few days, it may take as long as four weeks.

Note: some people have a different response to fibre than others. So it is very much trial and error as to what is most suitable for you. Some people report that a high-fibre diet or certain fibre supplements cause some persistent mild symptoms such as mild pains and bloating. This may be to do with the type of fibre being consumed. Insoluble fibre, found in cereals, wheat bran and nuts, may cause more wind and bloating. Eating a lot of bran-based foods or taking bran supplements can particularly aggravate symptoms in some people. Therefore, it may be helpful to have more soluble fibre (the type of fibre that can be dissolved in water), found mostly in fruit and vegetables. However, many foods contain both types of fibre, so when introducing a new high-fibre food, monitor your symptoms and adjust your diet accordingly.

Dietary sources of soluble fibre include oats, ispaghula (psyllium), nuts, flax seeds, lentils, beans, fruit and vegetables. A fibre supplement called ispaghula powder is also available from pharmacies and health food shops.

Insoluble fibre is chiefly found in corn (maize) bran, wheat bran, nuts and some fruit and vegetables.

What is the treatment for diverticulitis?

When symptoms are not too severe

If you develop diverticulitis you may need a course of antibiotic medicine if you feel generally unwell. Follow the diverticulosis diet recommendations unless otherwise advised by your doctor. You may need some strong painkillers for a while. If the infection is not too severe then symptoms may well settle with this treatment.

Diverticulitis when to go to hospital

If symptoms are severe or prolonged then you may need to be admitted to hospital. You may be given fluids directly into a vein via a drip (intravenous fluids). Antibiotics may be required, either in tablet form or intravenously. You may also need to have painkilling injections. You may also be admitted to hospital if the symptoms are not too severe but do not settle after a couple of days of treatment at home.

If complications develop

As mentioned earlier, some people with diverticulitis develop complications such as:

- Bowel blockage (obstruction).
- A collection of pus (an abscess).

- A channel (fistula) that may form to other organs.
- A tummy (abdominal) infection (peritonitis).

Surgery is usually needed to treat these serious but uncommon complications. For example, surgery is sometimes needed to drain an abscess or to remove a badly infected part of the colon.

Discharge instructions:

Return to the emergency department if:
- You have bowel movement or foul-smelling discharge leaking from your vagina or in your urine.
- You have severe diarrhea.
- You urinate less than usual or not at all.
- You are not able to have a bowel movement.
- You cannot stop vomiting.

- You have severe abdominal pain, a fever, and your abdomen is larger than usual.

- You have new or increased blood in your bowel movements.

- Call your doctor if:

- You have pain when you urinate.

- Your symptoms get worse or do not go away.

- You have questions or concerns about your condition or care.

Medicines:

Antibiotics may be given to help treat a bacterial infection.

Prescription pain medicine may be given. Ask your healthcare provider how to take this medicine safely. Some prescription pain medicines contain acetaminophen. Do not take other medicines that contain acetaminophen without talking to your healthcare provider. Too much acetaminophen may cause liver damage. Prescription pain medicine may cause constipation. Ask your healthcare provider how to prevent or treat constipation.

Take your medicine as directed. Contact your healthcare provider if you think your medicine is not helping or if you have side effects. Tell your provider if you are allergic to any medicine. Keep a list of the medicines, vitamins, and herbs you take. Include the amounts, and when and why you take them. Bring the list or the pill bottles to follow-up visits. Carry your medicine list with you in case of an emergency.

Treatment options
The following list of medications are in some way related to or used in the treatment of this condition.

- metronidazole
- Flagyl
- Cipro
- ciprofloxacin
- Bactrim DS

What is a diverticulitis diet?

A diverticulitis diet includes foods that allow your intestines to rest while you have diverticulitis. Diverticulitis is a condition that causes diverticula (small pockets) along your intestine to become inflamed or infected. This is caused by hard bowel movement, food, or bacteria that get stuck in the pockets.

Diverticula

Which foods may be recommended while I have diverticulitis?

A clear liquid diet may be recommended for 2 to 3 days. A clear liquid diet includes clear liquids, and foods that are liquid at room temperature. Examples include the following:

Water and clear juices (such as apple, cranberry, or grape), strained citrus juices or fruit punch

Coffee or tea (without cream or milk)

Clear sports drinks or soft drinks, such as ginger ale, lemon-lime soda, or club soda (no cola or root beer)

Clear broth, bouillon, or consommé

Plain popsicles (no popsicles with pureed fruit or fiber)

Flavored gelatin without fruit

Low-fiber foods may be recommended until your symptoms improve. Examples include the following:

Cream of wheat and finely ground grits

White bread, white pasta, and white rice

Canned and well-cooked fruit without skins or seeds, and juice without pulp

Canned and well-cooked vegetables without skins or seeds, and vegetable juice

Cow's milk, lactose-free milk, soy milk, and rice milk

Yogurt, cottage cheese, and sherbet

Eggs, poultry (such as chicken and turkey), fish, and tender, ground, well-cooked beef

Tofu and smooth nut butters, such as peanut butter

Broth and strained soups made of low-fiber foods
What do I need to know about high-fiber foods?

High-fiber foods can help prevent diverticulosis and diverticulitis. Your healthcare provider will tell you when you can add high-fiber foods back into your diet. Examples include the following:

Whole grains and breads, and cereals made with whole grains

Dried fruit, fresh fruit with skin, and fruit pulp

Raw vegetables

Cooked greens, such as spinach

Tough meat and meat with gristle

Legumes, such as pinto beans and lentils

1. Bean Enchiladas

Ingredients

14 Ounces can red beans, drained, rinsed, mashed

2 Cups cheddar cheese, grated

1/2 Cup onion, chopped

1/4 Cup black olives, sliced

2 Cups tomato sauce

2 Teaspoons garlic salt

8 whole wheat tortillas

Instructions

Preheat oven to 350F degrees.

In a medium bowl, combine the mashed beans, cheese, onions, olives, one cup tomato sauce, and garlic salt.

Place about 1/3 cup bean mixture along center of each tortilla. Roll up and place enchiladas in large baking dish.

Spoon remaining tomato sauce on top of the filled tortillas. Sprinkle with additional cheese, if desired.

Bake for 15 to 20 minutes or until thoroughly heated.

2. Beef and Penne Pasta Toss

Ingredients

1 Pound whole wheat penne pasta

1 Pound ground beef, lean

2 Tablespoons olive oil

1 small onion, chopped

3 garlic cloves, minced

15 Ounces can tomatoes, seeded, diced

2 Cups medium zucchini, seeded, chopped

8 Ounces fresh spinach, chopped

1 Cup Parmesan cheese, grated

Instructions

Bring a large pot of salted water to a boil. Cook penne pasta al dente according to package directions.

In a large non-stick pan, brown ground beef over medium-high heat for 6 to 8 minutes, breaking up any large pieces. Remove beef and set aside on paper towels to drain excess fat.

In the same pan, heat olive oil over medium-high heat. Cook onions and garlic for about 5 minutes or until soft. Add tomatoes and zucchini and continue cooking 5 minutes more. Add spinach and cook until it just wilts, 2-3 minutes. Return beef to skillet and stir in 1/2 cup cheese; heat through Transfer pasta to a large serving bowl and spoon meat mixture on top.

Toss until well combined and sprinkle with remaining cheese.

3. Beef Fajitas

Ingredients

6 Ounces flank steak, trimmed of fat

2 Teaspoons lime juice

1 Teaspoon garlic, chopped

1 Teaspoon olive oil, divided

15 Ounces can red beans, drained, rinsed, mashed

1/2 Cup medium green pepper, seeded and thinly sliced

1/2 Cup red bell pepper, thinly sliced

1 Tablespoon scallions, chopped

4 whole wheat tortillas

Instructions

Season flank steak with salt. Let sit for 10 minutes. Grill flank steak over high heat until cooked on both sides. Place steak on separate plate to rest for 10 minutes. Cut flank steak into thin strips against the grain.

In a small bowl, whisk together lime juice, garlic, and 1/2 teaspoon of olive oil. Set aside.

In a small pan, heat the other 1/2 tsp olive oil and combine beans, bell peppers and scallions and heat through.

To assemble fajitas, take tortilla and place steak inside. Top with bean mixture and drizzle some of the lime sauce on top.

Roll into fajita and serve immediately.

4. Black Bean Quesadillas

Ingredients

1 Tablespoon olive oil

1/2 small onion, chopped

1/2 Cup red bell pepper, seeded, chopped

1 clove, minced

28 Ounces black beans, rinsed, drained, lightly mashed

1/2 Teaspoon cumin

3 Tablespoons cilantro, chopped

1/4 Cup black olives, sliced

2 Cups fresh spinach, chopped

3/4 Cups Monterey Jack cheese, shredded

8 whole wheat tortillas

Instructions

Preheat oven to 350 degrees.

In a medium pan, heat olive oil over medium heat. Cook onions and red peppers until soft, about 5 minutes. Add garlic and continue to cook another 2 minutes, add mashed beans, cilantro and olives, and cumin and cook another 5 minutes to combine all ingredients.

Spread mixture evenly onto 4 tortillas. Sprinkle with spinach and cheese.

Top with remaining tortillas. Bake tortillas on ungreased cookie sheet for 12 minutes. Cut into wedges and serve.

5. Broccoli and Mushroom Brown Rice

Ingredients

1 Tablespoon olive oil

1 medium onion, chopped

2 garlic cloves, minced

1 Cup instant brown rice

8 Ounces Portobello mushrooms, sliced

3/4 Cups vegetable broth

1 Pound broccoli florets, fresh, cut into bite-size pieces

1/2 Teaspoon salt

1/4 Teaspoon pepper

Instructions

In a medium pan, heat olive oil over medium-high heat. Cook onions and garlic until translucent, about 5 minutes.

Stir in rice and mushrooms and cook 3-5 minutes or until mushrooms have released all of their juices. Add the broth and bring to a boil. Reduce heat to medium-low and cover until liquid is absorbed (about 7 - 8 minutes).

Place broccoli florets in a microwave-safe casserole dish and sprinkle with salt and pepper and add 4 tbs. water. Cover and cook at high power for 5 to 7 minutes or until tender.

Fluff rice with a fork and pour into a serving platter and top with broccoli. Toss to combine and serve. Can be topped with freshly grated Parmesan cheese and fresh Italian parsley.

6. Chicken and Asparagus Pasta

Ingredients

1 Pound whole wheat penne pasta

2 Tablespoons olive oil

1 Pound chicken breast halves, boneless and sliced into strips

1/2 Teaspoon poultry seasoning

4 Pieces garlic cloves, minced

1 1/2 Cup asparagus, frozen, thawed, cut into 1 inch pieces

1 Cup peas, frozen, thawed

1/4 Cup Parmesan cheese, grated

Instructions

Bring a large pot of salted water to boil. Add pasta and cook al dente according to package directions.

Heat one tablespoon olive oil in a pan over medium heat and cook chicken with poultry seasoning until golden. Remove cooked chicken from the pan.

Add the remaining tablespoon of olive oil, garlic, asparagus and peas. Cook until vegetables are tender.

Place chicken back in with the asparagus mixture and cook together for 2 minutes or until heated through.

Place pasta in a large shallow pasta bowl and toss with chicken mixture. Top with parmesan cheese.

7. Chicken and Avocado Pitas

Ingredients

2 Cups cooked chicken. chopped

1 avocado, medium, chopped

14 Ounces can red beans, drained, rinsed, mashed

1 Teaspoon lemon juice

1 Cup tomatoes, seeded, chopped

1 Cup cottage cheese

4 whole wheat pita pockets

Instructions

In a large mixing bowl, combine chicken, avocado, red beans, lemon juice, tomatoes, and cottage cheese.

Slice the pita bread to make a pocket and spoon in the chicken mixture. Serve.

8. Chicken Florentine

Ingredients

2 Tablespoons olive oil

2 zucchinis, seeded, thinly sliced

1/2 Cup green onion, sliced

2 chicken breast, cubed

1/2 Teaspoon salt

1/2 Teaspoon thyme, ground

3 Cups long grain rice, cooked

4 Cups fresh spinach, chopped

1/4 Cup Parmesan cheese, grated

Instructions

In a medium pan, heat olive oil over medium heat.

Add zucchini, onions, and chicken, stirring occasionally for 5 to 10 minutes, or until chicken is golden.

Add salt, thyme, rice and spinach. Cook and stir for another 6 - 8 minutes or until heated through and spinach wilts.

Remove from heat, transfer to a large serving bowl, and stir in cheese. Serve.

9. Chipotle Black Bean Chili

Ingredients

1 Tablespoon olive oil

1 Cup onion, finely chopped

garlic cloves, minced

1/2 Teaspoon chipotle powder

1/2 Teaspoon cumin

1/4 Teaspoon salt

30 Ounces can black beans, drained and rinsed

28 Ounces tomatoes, seeded, chopped

1 Teaspoon fresh cilantro

Instructions

In a large non-stick pan, heat olive oil over medium heat.

Add onions and garlic and cook 5 minutes or until they are soft. Add chipotle powder, cumin, salt, beans, and tomatoes bring to a boil.

Reduce heat, cover and simmer 15-25 or until chili thickens.

Garnish with fresh cilantro.

10. Cottage Crunch Wraps

Ingredients

3/4 Cups cottage cheese

1/4 Cup carrots, shredded

green onion, sliced

1/2 Cup tomatoes, seeded, chopped

1/2 Cup cabbage, chopped

1 Teaspoon lime juice

whole wheat tortillas

Instructions

In a medium bowl, place cheese, carrots, onions, tomatoes, and cabbage and mix well. Add lime juice. Place mixture in tortillas, wrap and serve.

11. Couscous with Chicken

Ingredients

4 Tablespoons olive oil

1 Pound chicken thighs, sliced into strips

onion, chopped

garlic cloves, minced

1 Cup carrots, shredded

1 Teaspoon smoked paprika

1 Teaspoon cumin

1/8 Teaspoon cinnamon

1/2 Teaspoon salt

1 Cup dried fruits, chopped (apricots, dates)

4 Cups chicken broth

2 Tablespoons butter

1 1/2 Cup couscous

1/2 Cup Italian parsley, chopped

Instructions

In a large, deep pan, heat oil over medium-high heat.

Cook chicken and brown 3 to 4 minutes on each side. Add onions, garlic, carrots, and season with spices and salt. Cook 6-8 minutes.

Stir the fruits into the chicken and vegetables, and 2 1/2 cups of stock. Allow to boil. Reduce heat to low, cover and simmer 10 minutes.

In a separate small saucepan, over medium heat, pour 1 1/2 cups stock and bring up to a boil then stir in couscous.

Remove from heat, cover and let stand 5 minutes. Fluff with fork and serve with chicken.

12. Couscous with Vegetables

Ingredients

1 1/2 Cup chicken broth

1 Cup couscous

4 Tablespoons olive oil, divided

red onion, chopped

garlic cloves, minced

tomatoes, seeded, chopped

yellow bell pepper, seeded and chopped

red bell pepper, seeded and chopped

zucchinis, seeded, chopped

1 Cup peas, thawed from frozen

2 Tablespoons balsamic vinegar

2 Tablespoons Feta cheese, crumbled

Instructions

In a medium saucepan, over high heat, bring chicken broth and 1 tbs of olive oil to a boil. Remove from heat and stir in couscous. Cover and let sit for 5-10 minutes.

In a separate pan over medium heat, add the remaining oil and cook the onions and garlic until softened.

Mix in the tomatoes, bell peppers and zucchinis. Cook and stir until tender.

Add peas and cook 2-3 more minutes. Add vinegar and cheese and toss to combine.

Spoon vegetable mixture over couscous. Serve.

13. Easy Turkey Chili

Ingredients

3 Tablespoons olive oil

garlic cloves, minced

onion, chopped

1 Pound ground turkey

Bay leaf

1 Teaspoon ground cumin

1 Teaspoon dried oregano

tomato, seeded, chopped

14 Ounces can tomato sauce

1 Cup beef broth

1 Teaspoon salt

28 Ounces can red beans, drained and rinsed

Instructions

In a large pot, heat oil over medium heat and cook garlic and onions for a 5 minutes.

Increase heat to high and add turkey, bay leaf, cumin and oregano. Cook until turkey has browned, about 5-7 minutes.

Add tomato, tomato sauce, broth and salt. Bring pot to a boil and then lower heat to simmer. Cover and simmer for about 20 minutes.

Add beans and more water if needed, and continue to simmer for 25 more minutes. Serve.

14. Garbanzo Pita Pockets

Ingredients

15 Ounces can garbanzo beans, drained, rinsed

6 Ounces can artichokes, marinated, quartered, liquid reserved

1 Tablespoon black olives. sliced

1 Tablespoon green olives, sliced

green bell pepper, seeded, chopped

red bell pepper, seeded and chopped

small red onion, thinly sliced

2 Tablespoons red wine vinegar

1/2 Cup fresh basil, chopped

whole wheat pita pockets

Instructions

In a large bowl, combine the garbanzo beans, artichokes and their liquid, olives, garlic, peppers, onion, vinegar and basil. Mix well and set aside.

Slice pita bread to make a pocket. Place a lettuce leaf in each pita and fill with the garbanzo filling. Serve.

15. Apple Chicken Pita Pocket

Ingredients

2 Cups chicken, cooked, cubed

2 apples, unpeeled, chopped

1 celery stalk, chopped

1/3 Cup plain yogurt

1/4 Cup mayonaise

4 round whole wheat pita breads

4 romaine lettuce leaves

Instructions

In a medium bowl, combine the chicken, apples, and celery.

Add yogurt and mayonnaise. Mix well. Slice pita to make a pocket.

Line with lettuce leaf and fill pita pocket with 1 cup of mixture per pita bread.

Serve with mixed fruit salad (no berries).

16. Aromatic Rice with Lentils

Ingredients

2 Tablespoons olive oil

1 onion, chopped

2 carrots, chopped

1 red bell pepper, seeded and chopped

2 garlic cloves, minced

1 Tablespoon fresh basil, chopped

1 Tablespoon fresh oregano, chopped

1/2 Tablespoon fresh sage, chopped

1 Cup brown rice

3 Cups chicken broth

1 Cup lentils, uncooked and rinsed

Instructions

In a large pan, heat olive oil over medium-high heat. Cook onion, carrot and pepper until softened, about 5-7 minutes.

Add garlic and cook for one more minute. Add basil, oregano, sage and rice. Stir to combine.

Stir in broth. Bring to a boil, stirring occasionally. Add lentils. Cover and reduce heat to low and let simmer for 20-25 minutes.

Fluff with fork and serve.

17. Bean and Mushroom Stew

Ingredients

2 Tablespoons olive oil

1 Pound white mushrooms, sliced

1 Cup onion, chopped

1 Teaspoon garlic cloves, minced

3/4 Teaspoons dried thyme

28 Ounces chicken broth

14 Ounces can stewed tomatoes, chopped

1/4 Cup white wine, optional

30 Ounces can,cannellini beans, drained and rinsed

Instructions

In a large saucepan, heat olive oil over medium high heat. Cook mushrooms, onion, garlic and thyme until onion is tender and mushrooms are slightly golden (about 7 minutes).

Add chicken broth, tomatoes and wine and bring to a boil. Cover and simmer for about 35 additional minutes.

In a small bowl, mash 1 cup of the beans until smooth; add to stew. Stir in remaining beans, heat until hot.

Serve immediately with a side of cooked long grain rice, if desired.

18. Bean and Vegetable Casserole

Ingredients

3 Tablespoons vegetable oil

1 large onion, chopped

2 celery stalks, chopped

1 medium green pepper, seeded and diced

2 medium tomatoes, seeded and chopped

2 Cups red kidney beans, drained and rinsed

1 Cup cannellini beans, drained and rinsed

1 Cup barley

2/3 Cups Italian parsley, chopped

1/2 Teaspoon salt

1 Teaspoon Italian seasoning

1 Teaspoon cumin

1 3/4 Cup boiling water

Instructions

Preheat oven to 350F degrees.

In a large non-stick pan, heat oil over medium-high heat. Add onion, celery, and green pepper. Cook for 10 minutes or until vegetables soften.

Stir in tomatoes, kidney beans, cannellini beans, barley, parsley, salt, Italian seasoning, and cumin.

Transfer mixture to a 2-to 3 quart casserole that has been sprayed with non-stick cooking spray.

Add boiling water. Cover. Bake at 350 degrees for 1-1/2 hours or until barley is tender and liquid is absorbed.

19. Summer Spaghetti

Ingredients

1 Pound whole wheat spaghetti

1/4 Cup olive oil

shallot, minced

garlic cloves, minced

medium zucchini, chopped

medium summer squash, chopped

1/4 Cup fresh basil, chopped

1/2 Teaspoon salt

medium lemon, juiced

2 Tablespoons butter, room temperature

freshly grated lemon peel

Instructions

Bring a large pot of salted water to boil. Add pasta and cook according to package directions until al dente.

In a large pan, heat oil over medium heat and cook the shallot and garlic stirring frequently.

Add the zucchini, squash, and basil. Continue to cook, stirring occasionally, until all vegetables are tender. Season with salt and lemon juice.

Immediately place the sautéed vegetables with all their juices in a large shallow pasta bowl.

Add the linguine and butter, toss to mix well and serve immediately. Top with freshly grated lemon peel.

20. Grilled Fish Tacos

Ingredients

1/4 Teaspoon salt

lemon, juiced

2 Tablespoons olive oil

fish filets, trout or tilapia

1/2 Cup red onion, chopped

1/2 Cup jicama, peeled, chopped

1/3 Cup red bell pepper, seeded and chopped

2/3 Cups fresh cilantro, finely chopped

1 Cup black beans, drained, rinsed

lime, zest and juice

1 Tablespoon plain yogurt

whole wheat tortillas

Instructions

In a small bowl, combine salt, lemon juice, and olive oil. Pour mixture over fish fillets and let marinate for 10 minutes.

Grill fish over high heat until cooked through, about 3 minutes per side.

In a separate bowl, combine onion, jicama, bell pepper, cilantro, beans, zest and juice of lime and yogurt to make a "salsa".

To make tacos, place fish in warmed tortilla and cover with "salsa" and fold in half. Serve.

21. Grilled Steak with Spinach and Apple Salad

Ingredients

beef steaks, rib-eye or sirloin

4 Tablespoons olive oil

salt and pepper to taste

1 Tablespoon balsamic vinegar

2 Cups fresh baby spinach, washed and dried

apple (preferably tart, like Granny Smith), unpeeled and sliced

4 Ounces Parmesan cheese, grated

Instructions

Prepare steaks for grill by pouring 2 tbs olive oil and salt to taste. Grill over high heat to desired doneness, about 7 minutes per side for medium. Once cooked, place steaks on plate to rest and let juices redistribute without cutting.

To make dressing, in a small bowl, whisk together balsamic vinegar, 2 tbs olive oil and salt and pepper to taste.

n individual plates, stack spinach, apples and steak that have been cut diagonally. Drizzle with dressing and top with Parmesan cheese.

22. Grilled Vegetable Quesadilla

Ingredients

zucchini, sliced in half, lengthwise

yello squash, sliced in half lengthwise

onion, sliced in fourths, lenghtwise

red pepper, seeded and quartered

Portobello mushroom cap

1/2 Teaspoon Italian seasoning

1/4 Teaspoon salt

whole wheat tortillas

1/2 Cup Mozzarella cheese, shredded

Instructions

Grill vegetables over medium heat until all of the vegetables are cooked. Season with Italian seasoning and salt. Slice vegetables and toss together.

Heat a pan sprayed with non-stick cooking spray over medium heat and place one tortilla in the pan. Spread some of the vegetable mixture over the tortilla, sprinkle with cheese and top with the remaining tortilla. Turn tortilla over and heat the other side until cheese melts but do not brown the tortillas. Serve.

23. Grilled Veggie Sandwich

Ingredients

eggplant, sliced in half-inch thick slices

zucchini, sliced in half-inch thick slices

red pepper, seeded and quartered

portobello mushroom caps

1/2 Cup olive oil

1/4 Teaspoon salt

1 Cup goat cheese

8 Ounces whole wheat crusty bread like baguette

1 Cup fresh baby spinach, washed and dried

Instructions

With a pastry brush, brush olive oil on the vegetable slices and the mushrooms caps. Season them with salt.

Place vegetables on a hot grill and cook until they are tender. To assemble, slice mushrooms into 1/4-inch slices, spread both sides of the bread with goat cheese and then top with 1 slice each of grilled vegetables and a quarter of the mushrooms.

Top with spinach and remaining piece of bread. Serve.

24. Lentil Linguine Stew

Ingredients

3 Tablespoons olive oil

onion, chopped

garlic cloves, minced

carrots, chopped

celery stalks, chopped

1 Cup lentils, uncooked, rinsed

6 Cups vegetable broth

4 Cups water

2 Teaspoons salt

bay leaves

1/2 Cup linguine, cut into 1-inch pieces

2 Cups kale, chopped

1/2 Cup Italian parsley, chopped

Instructions

In a large pot, heat olive oil over moderate heat.
Cook the onion, garlic, and carrots and celery for
10 minutes, stirring occasionally, until tender.

Add the lentils, broth, water, salt, and bay leaf
to the pot. Bring to a boil. Reduce the heat and
simmer, partially covered, stirring occasionally,
for 25 minutes.

Add the linguine and simmer, stirring
occasionally, until the lentils are tender and the
pasta and kale are tender, 15 to 20 minutes
longer.

Stir parsley into the stew. Serve.

25. Lentil Risotto

Ingredients

2 Tablespoons olive oil

medium leeks, chopped

garlic cloves, minced

red bell pepper, seeded and chopped

3 Cups chicken broth

1 1/4 Cup long grain rice

1 Tablespoon fresh basil, chopped

1 Cup lentils, cooked

1/4 Cup Italian parsley, chopped

1/4 Cup Parmesan cheese, grated

Instructions

In a large pot, heat olive oil over moderate heat and cook leeks, garlic, and red pepper until softened.

Add broth along with the rice, and basil. Cover and let simmer until rice is done then add cooked lentils and stir for 10 minutes.

Remove from heat and add parsley and parmesan cheese. Serve.

26. Lentil Stew

Ingredients

1 Tablespoon vegetable oil

1 onion, chopped

2 garlic cloves, minced

1 green bell pepper, seeded, chopped

2 Cups kale, chopped

3 Cups vegetable broth

1 1/4 Cup lentils, uncooked, rinsed

15 Ounces can tomato sauce

1 Tablespoon Italian seasoning

1/2 Teaspoon paprika

Instructions

In a large saucepan, heat oil over medium-high heat. Cook onion, garlic, and bell pepper, stirring frequently, until vegetables are tender. Stir in water, lentils, tomato sauce and spices. Reduce heat to low and partially cover and simmer 35 to 40 minutes or until lentils are tender. Serve.

27. Pasta with Beans and Turkey

Ingredients

1 Pound whole wheat pasta

1 Tablespoon olive oil

onion

garlic cloves, minced

1 Pound ground turkey

small head escarole, rinsed, drained, and chopped

14 Ounces can,cannellini beans, drained and rinsed

1 1/2 Cup chicken broth

1 Tablespoon fresh rosemary, chopped

1/2 Teaspoon salt

1/2 Teaspoon pepper

1/2 Cup Parmesan cheese

Instructions

Bring a large pot of salted water to boil. Add pasta and cook according to package directions. Drain.

In a large pan, heat olive oil over medium heat.

Add onion and cook until softened, add garlic and turkey and cook until it browns, about 5-7 minutes.

Add the escarole and cook until wilted, about 3 to 4 minutes. Add the beans, 1 cup of chicken stock, rosemary, and salt and pepper. Simmer until the mixture is slightly thickened.

Add the turkey-bean mixture to pasta and toss well, thinning sauce with the additional 1/2 cup chicken stock if necessary.

Top with parmesan cheese. Serve.

28. Pasta with Chicken and Olives

Ingredients

1 Pound whole wheat pasta

2 Tablespoons olive oil

onion, chopped

garlic cloves, minced

1 Pound chicken breast, cut into chunks

1 Teaspoon dried basil

1 Teaspoon dried rosemary

black olives, sliced

green bell pepper, seeded, chopped

14 Ounces can stewed tomatoes, chopped

2 Cups chicken broth

1/2 Cup Romano cheese

Instructions

Bring a large pot of salted water to boil. Add pasta and cook according to package directions until al dente.

While pasta is cooking, heat the oil in a large pan over medium heat. Add the onion and garlic and cook until the onion is tender, about 6 minutes. Add the chicken, basil and rosemary and cook until the chicken is lightly browned, about 8 minutes. Stir in the olives, green pepper and tomatoes and cook until the tomatoes begin to give off liquid, about 2 minutes.

Add the chicken broth to the pan, heat pan to boiling and boil until half of the liquid is evaporated, about 5-7 minutes.

When pasta is done, add to sauce mixture. Toss until pasta is evenly mixed with sauce. Top with cheese and serve.

29. Pasta with Spinach and White Beans

Ingredients

1 Pound whole wheat pasta

2 Tablespoons olive oil

garlic cloves, minced

3 Cups tomatoes, seeded and chopped

14 Ounces can,cannellini beans, drained and rinsed

1 Cup tomato sauce

2 Cups fresh spinach, washed and chopped

1/2 Cup Feta cheese, crumbled

Instructions

Bring a large pot of water to a boil. Add salt and add pasta and cook according to package instructions. Drain.

In a large pan, heat olive oil over medium heat. Cook garlic for 3 - 4 minutes. Add tomatoes, beans and tomato sauce. Bring to a boil. Reduce heat, cover and let simmer for 20 minutes.

Add spinach to the sauce and let simmer for another 5 minutes or until spinach wilts. Place cooked pasta in a large serving bowl, pour sauce over pasta and sprinkle feta cheese. Toss to combine. Serve.

30. Quick Broccoli Pasta Toss

Ingredients

2 Cups broccoli florets, fresh or thawed if frozen

1/2 p Pound whole wheat pasta

1/2 Tablespoon olive oil

1 1/2 Tablespoon Parmesan cheese

1/8 Teaspoon garlic powder

Instructions

Bring a large pot of salted water to a boil.

Add broccoli and pasta and cook for about 6 - 8 minutes or until tender. Drain well.

Place pasta mixture in a large shallow pasta bowl and toss with olive oil, cheese and garlic powder. Serve.

31. Red Beans and Rice

Ingredients

1 Tablespoon olive oil

onion, chopped

stalks celery, chopped

garlic cloves, minced

14 Ounces tomato sauce

1/2 Teaspoon oregano

1/2 Tablespoon thyme

14 Ounces beef stock

28 Ounces red beans, drained and rinsed

4 Cups cooked brown rice

Instructions

In a large non-stick pan, heat olive oil over medium heat. Cook onions, celery and garlic stirring until just tender.

Stir in tomato paste, oregano and thyme. Add beef broth, stir and bring to a boil. Simmer uncovered about 35 minutes or until mixture thickens. Add red beans and let cook until heated through.

Serve over brown rice.

32. Rice and Vegetable Casserole

Ingredients

Non-stick cooking spray

1 Cup long-grain brown rice

1/4 Cup mushrooms, sliced

1/4 Cup broccoli, chopped

1/4 Cup carrots, chopped

1/4 Cup red bell pepper, seeded and chopped

1/4 Cup onion, finely chopped

1 Teaspoon salt

1 Teaspoon paprika

1 Teaspoon oregano

2-2 1/2 Cups vegetable broth

1/4 Cup cheddar cheese, shredded

Instructions

Preheat oven to 425 degrees. Spray a 13x9 glass baking dish lightly with non-stick cooking spray.

In a large bowl, combine brown rice, mushrooms, broccoli, carrots, bell pepper, onion, salt, paprika, oregano, and broth. Mix well until all ingredients are incorporated. Transfer the mixture into the greased 13x9 baking dish and cover with foil.

Bake casserole dish in preheated oven for 30 minutes, or until cooked through; stir once half way during baking.

Top with shredded cheddar cheese and allow it to melt prior to serving.

33. Rice, Shrimp and Peas Bowl

Ingredients

1 Cup long-grain brown rice

1/4 Cup soy sauce, low sodium preferred

2 Tablespoons rice vinegar

1/4 Cup lemon juice

2 Tablespoons honey

1 Tablespoon olive oil

1 Pound medium shrimp, cleaned, peeled and deveined

8 Ounces snow peas, cut in halves

ginger piece, 1 inch long, shredded

avocado, sliced

Instructions

In a large saucepan, bring 2 cups of water to a boil. Add the rice and cover and reduce heat to simmer. Cook until rice is tender and water has evaporated, about 35-45 minutes.

While rice is cooking, in a small bowl, combine soy sauce, lemon juice, vinegar, and honey until well combined and set aside.

In a large non-stick pan, heat olive oil over medium-high heat. Cook shrimp with peas and ginger until shrimp turn pink, about 3-4 minutes.

To serve, place rice on plate and top with shrimp mixture and chopped avocado. Serve the sauce on the side.

34. Roasted Chicken and Vegetables

Ingredients

Roma tomatoes, seedless, quartered

zucchini, medium, chopped coarsely

potatoes, large, unpeeled, quartered

3 Tablespoons olive oil, divided

3/4 Teaspoons salt, divided

garlic cloves, minced

1 Tablespoon fresh rosemary, chopped

1 Tablespoon fresh thyme, taken off sprig

1 Teaspoon lemon zest

1 Tablespoon lemon juice

chicken breast halves, skinless

Instructions

Preheat oven to 375F degrees.

Place tomatoes, zucchini and potatoes in a large roasting pan, and toss with 2 tbs of oil and 1/4 tsp salt.

In a small bowl, combine 1 tbs oil, 1/2 tsp salt, garlic, rosemary, thyme, lemon zest and lemon juice.

Pour this mixture over chicken. Place chicken in pan with vegetables. Bake in oven for 30 minutes.

Stir chicken and vegetables and bake another 25 minutes, or until chicken is cooked through and vegetables are tender.

35. Shrimp and Black Bean Nachos

Ingredients

3/4 Cups cilantro,chopped

1/2 Cup red onion, diced

2 Tablespoons lemon juice

1 Tablespoon olive oil

1 Teaspoon Worcestershire Sauce

1/2 Teaspoon salt

1 Pound shrimp, peeled and cooked and chopped

2 Cups tomatoes, seeded, diced

1/2 Cup avocado, diced

15 Ounces black beans, drained and rinsed

1/2 Teaspoon cumin

4 Cups baked tortilla chips

Instructions

Combine cilantro, onion, lime juice, oil, Worcestershire sauce, salt and shrimp in a large bowl; toss well.

Cover and refrigerate for 30 minutes. Add tomato and avocado; stir well.

Place the beans and cumin in a food processor, and process 30 seconds or until smooth.

Spread each chip with 1-teaspoon black-bean mixture.

Top with 1-tablespoon shrimp mixture. Serve

36. Southwestern Chicken Pitas

Ingredients

15 Ounces black beans, drained and rinsed

1/2 Cup red bell pepper, seeded and chopped

3 Tablespoons fresh lemon juice

2 Tablespoons fersh cilantro, minced

2 Teaspoons olive oil

chicken breast halves, skinless

round whole wheat pita pockets

Monterrey Jack cheese, slices

Instructions

In a bowl, combine beans, bell pepper, lime juice, and cilantro. Set aside.

In a large pan, heat canola oil over medium-high heat. Cook chicken in pan until golden brown. Set aside for 10 without cutting.

Warm pita bread in oven. Cut chicken into slices. For each sandwich, place cheese slice halves down center of one pita bread.

Top with chicken breast slices and bean mixture. Roll up tightly. Cut in half and serve.

37. Spaghetti with Zucchini

Ingredients

1 Pound whole wheat spaghetti

2 zucchini, grated, water squeezed out or spiraled

2 Tablespoons butter

1 Tablespoon olive oil

garlic cloves, minced

1/2 Cup Parmesan cheese, grated

Instructions

Bring a large pot of salted water to boil. Add pasta and cook according to package directions until al dente.

While pasta is cooking, in a large non-stick pan, heat butter and oil together. Add grated zucchini and cook for about 3 minutes. Add garlic and cook for one more minute, stirring constantly. Add 1/4 cup of grated parmesan cheese.

Place pasta in a large shallow pasta bowl and toss in zucchini mixture. Top with remaining parmesan cheese. Serve

38. Spinach and Ham Pizza

Ingredients

1 store bought baked thin crust whole wheat pizza shell

4 Cups baby spinach leaves, sliced thinly

1/2 Cup Mushrooms

2 Tablespoons olive oil

3 Ounces ham or prosciutto

1/4 Cup feta cheese, crumbled

1/4 Cup Parmesan cheese, grated

3 Pieces garlic cloves, sliced thinly

Instructions

Preheat oven to 450F degrees.

Place the pizza shell on a cookie sheet. Scatter spinach and mushrooms all over crust. Drizzle with oil. Place ham or prosciutto, cheeses, and garlic on top of spinach & mushroom.

Bake for 10-12 minutes, until crust is golden brown and spinach is wilted.

Conclusion

See a doctor if you have a change in the pattern of your toilet habit. For example, a sudden change from your normal bowel habit to persisting constipation or diarrhoea, passing blood or mucus, or new pains. Even if you are known to have diverticula, a change of symptoms may indicate a new and different gut (intestinal) problem. Call an ambulance urgently if you have a large amount of bleeding from the bowel.

Printed in Great Britain
by Amazon

16125899R00051